FERRARIS AT LE MANS

DOMINIQUE PASCAL

Foulis

Haynes

ISBN 0 85429 492 9

A FOULIS Motoring Book

This edition first published 1986

© E.P.A., Paris 1984

Published by:
Haynes Publishing Group
Sparkford, Nr. Yeovil, Somerset BA22
7JJ, England

Haynes Publications Inc.
861 Lawrence Drive, Newbury Park,
California 91320 USA

British Library Cataloguing in Publication Data

Ferraris at Le Mans.
  1. Ferrari automobile–History
  I. Pascal, Dominique
  629.2'28   TL215.F47
  ISBN 0–85429–492–9

Library of Congress catalog card number

85–82313

Contents

'. . . a happy blend of function and line that recalls the sublime work of Leonardo da Vinci, of which Ferrari is a worthy successor. . .'

U.W.

Ferrari at Le Mans is the story of this marque's entries, either direct or through private teams, in this fantastic event which demands so much of machines and men.

Heat, cold, fear, fatigue, dust or rain – all of these contrast with the comfort of the normal lives of these people: drivers, mechanics or spectators.

To have drawn them all to Le Mans for more than half a century there have had to be many top liners, and Ferrari is not the least of these.

How many times have the media headlined duels between Ferrari and Talbot, Ferrari and Jaguar, Ferrari and Ford, Ferrari and Porsche – and even between private and works Ferraris!

This glorious marque from beyond the Alps is no stranger to England or France, and the relationship is reciprocal.

May all the protagonists in this extraordinary event find in this book the homage that is their due.

D.P.

1949

After a gap of 10 years the Le Mans 24 Hours was starting up again. Centre stage at this first post-war event were two small red racers from a new Italian marque, one of which was to win. The Ferrari 166 MM (for Mille Miglia) was a competition car that the little firm sold to its sporting customers.

Ferrari no. 22. Type 166 MM (chassis no. 0008), entered by Lord Selsdon, driven by Chinetti and Selsdon. It was placed first in the distance classification, having covered 3178.299km (1974.903 miles) in 24 hours at an average 132.420km/h (82.282mph).

First in distance, first in its 1500–2000cc class, first in the Index of Performance, the first participation of Ferrari at Le Mans, the first victory for a V12 there – but the lap record escaped it and went to André Simon in a Delahaye (5' 12.5sec).

In his leather helmet and aviator's goggles, Luigi Chinetti, the Italian-American with a French heart, drove his Ferrari solo for 22 hours, paying careful attention to his deficient clutch and putting himself a reasonable distance in front of the Delage of Louveau and Jover, which came in second. In that year Chinetti and Selsdon wrote one of the finest pages in the Ferrari story at the Le Mans circuit. However, they did not beat the record for the course set up in 1939 by Wimille and Veyron in a Bugatti: 3354.760km (2084.551 miles). Note that the engine of this 166 MM developed 160hp at 6600rpm. The intermediate placings of Ferrari number 22 were third in the third hour; second in the sixth hour and first from the ninth to the finish.

Ferrari no. 23. Type 166 MM, driven by Ferret and Lucas. It withdrew on the 53rd lap. The retirement of this second Ferrari was caused when it left the road. It was slightly faster than the winning car. Ferret, alias the famous banker Pierre-Louis Dreyfus, was an associate of Jean Lucas, who later founded the magazine *Sport-Auto*. At the end of the first three hours they were in fourth place behind the two Delahayes and the other Ferrari. The car was going well when Dreyfus lost control on the Maison-Blanche bends, damaging the beautiful Touring coachwork.

This was the first time the company took part in the event. It won – and linked its name for ever with this corner of France.

1950

Five Ferraris start, none finish

Annoyed by its 1949 setback, Talbot assigned two Formula One cars converted into two-seaters to this year's Le Mans. The winner, Louis Rosier, drove for the 24 hours except for two laps which he left to his son Jean-Louis.

The victorious team of Louis and Jean-Louis Rosier in their Talbot-Lago covered 4483km (2785.207 miles) at an average of 144.380km/h (89.714 mph).

Ferrari no. 24. Type 195 S, driven by Chinette and 'Heldé'. It withdrew in the 19th hour after being in 32nd place in the preceding hour. 'Heldé' was another alias for Pierre-Louis Dreyfus who this time was partnering the three-times Le Mans winner.
At midnight their sports car was ony two laps behind the Rosier Talbot – the latter drove the single-seater for more than 23 hours (his son did only two laps). The rear axle and the transmission packed up and Chinetti got back to the pits, on foot, at 10am. His best placing had been second in the fourth, fifth, seventh and eighth hours.

Ferrari no. 28. Type 166 MM, entered by Lord Selsdon, driven by Lucas and Selsdon. It withdrew in the 17th hour.

Lord Selsdon drove only a few laps at Le Mans the previous year, although it was his car that won the event. He intended to make up for this in 1950 but unfortunately Jean Lucas left the road at the Tertre-Rouge. The car's best position was sixth in the 14th, 15th and 16th hours of the event.

Ferrari no. 25. Type 195 S, driven by Sommer and Serafini. It withdrew in the 12th hour.

This was the first Ferrari saloon in 'French Blue' to race at Le Mans. Sommer made a dazzling start, taking the lap record with a speed of 165.470km/h (102.818 mph). At the end of the first two hours the car was lying first but subsequently dropped back. A broken dynamo mounting forced this brilliant team to retire.

Ferrari no. 26. Type 166 MM, driven by Rubirosa and Leygonie. It withdrew in the eighth hour.

Their best place was eighth in the second hour before the clutch showed signs of fatigue, finally obliging them to give up around midnight.

Ferrari no. 27. Type 166 MM, driven by Yvonne Simon and Kasse. It withdrew in the sixth hour.

These two ladies were the first women drivers to compete at Le Mans in a Ferrari (Yvonne Simon returned to the Sarthe circuit in 1951 in partnership with Miss Haig). Quite early on Yvonne left the road at Mulsanne and stuck in the sand and had to dig herself out with a shovel. Unfortunately, repeated use of the accelerator in freeing herself used the last of her fuel and she finally had to give up with an empty tank. The best placing of this team was 29th in the second hour.

1951

Nine Ferraris start, four finish

As with Ferrari two years earlier, it was once again a new marque that made itself felt in the general classification: Jaguar. Another quite young marque also achieved its first class success with its first participation – this was Porsche.

Another first for Ferrari was the arrival at the finish of a female team in a little 166 MM. The winners of the event were P. Walker and P. Whitehead in a Jaguar XK120C; they covered 3611.193km (2243.891 miles) at an average 150.466km/h (93.495mph).

Ferrari no. 15. Type 340 America (chassis no. 0124), entered by Luigi Chinetti, driven by Chinetti and Lucas. It came eighth on distance, covering 3328.160km (2068.003 miles) at an average 138.673km/h (86.167mph).
Like the other three 340 Americas, this sports car had coachwork by Touring.

Ferrari no. 29. Type 212 Export, entered by N. Mahé, driven by Mahé and Péron. It was placed ninth on distance, covering 3297.420km (2048.922 miles) at an average 137.392km/h (85.371 mph).

Ferrari no. 32. Type 166 MM, entered by Luigi Chinetti, driven by Mme Simon and Miss Haig. It came in 15th on distance, covering 3124.690km (1941.592 miles) at an average 130.195km/h (80.899mph).
These ladies finished the event creditably in the car that had stuck in the sand the previous year.

11

Ferrari no. 31. Type 212 Export (chassis no. 067), entered by Moran, driven by Moran and Cornacchia. It came in 16th place on distance, covering 3072.180km (1908.964 miles) at an average 128.006km/h (79.540mph).

Ferrari no. 30. Type 212 Export, entered by Larivière, driven by Larivière and Guelfi. Larivière died in an accident at the Tertre-Rouge when his car ran off the circuit.

Ferrari no. 18. Type 340 America, entered by E. R. Hall, driven by Hall and Navone. It retired with starter trouble.

Ferrari no. 17. Type 340 America, entered by Spear, driven by Spear and Claes. It withdrew with clutch trouble.

Ferrari no. 16. Type 340 America, entered by Luigi Chinetti, driven by Chiron and 'Heldé'.
This car was disqualified for refuelling early.

Ferrari no. 64. Type 166 MM, entered by R. A. Bouchard, driven by Bouchard and Farnaud.
This was the first of the Ferraris to retire.

13

1952

Seven Ferraris start, one finishes

Talbot attempted a come-back this year, as did Mercedes: the German marque took the prize. Levegh in a Talbot, who was winning, had engine failure 70 minutes from the finish. Note that the Frenchmen Simon and Vincent in their new Ferrari 340 America led the field for two hours in succession.

The winning team, Lang and Riess in a Mercedes 300 SL, covered 3733.800km (2320.076 miles) at an average 155.575km/h (96.670mh).

Ferrari no. 14. Type 340 America (chassis no. 0206), entered by Luigi Chinetti, driven by Simon and Vincent. It came fifth on distance, covering 3361.810km (2088.932 miles) at an average 140.078km/h (87.040mph).
This was the only Ferrari to finish out of seven – the biggest entry in the event so far.
After a sensational start which saw the car in the lead at the end of the first two hours, this blue saloon, with bodywork by Vignale, experienced its first difficulties, which pushed it back to 17th place. Thanks to the skill of its drivers it climbed back to a brilliant fifth place, only 27 laps behind the winning Mercedes.

Ferrari no. 12. Type 340 America (chassis no. 0204), entered by Luigi Chinetti, driven by Chinetti and Lucas. It was disqualified in the 13th hour, after being in seventh place in the preceding hour.

Luigi Chinetti was disqualified for not observing the rule concerning 28 laps between refuelling. This is a cast-iron regulation at Le Mans and this second Vignale-bodied Spyder was obliged to retire. Consistent driving had kept it in fifth place from the 6th to the 11th hours.

Ferrari no. 33. Type 212 Export, driven by Moran and Cornacchia. It withdrew in the 12th hour, after being in 32nd position in the previous hour.

This Vignale saloon retired with electrical faults. Its best placing had been 25th in the fifth hour and its worst 54th at the beginning of the race.

15

Ferrari no. 30. Type 225 S, driven by Pagnibon and Cole. It retired in the 11th hour after being in 32nd place in the previous hour. Another Vignale saloon, it had been in 15th place in the third hour.

Ferrari no. 15. Type 340 America, entered by Ecurie France, driven by Rosier and Trintignant. It withdrew in the sixth hour, after being in 12th place the previous hour.
A crack team for this car (which Taruffi drove in the Mille Miglia), they succeeded in getting it into third place in the general classification for a short while before troubles began.

Ferrari no. 16. Type 340 America, entered by Pierre-Louis Dreyfus, driven by Dreyfus-'Heldé'. It retired in the fifth hour, after being in 40th position in the preceding hour. The clutch of this Touring-bodied tourer began to slip after three hours, although it had not been placed higher than 13th.

Ferrari no. 62. Type 250 S (chassis no. 0156), driven by Ascari and Villoresi. It retired in the third hour having been in 43rd position in the preceding hour.

This was the first Ferrari to retire, after an impressive start which clearly showed the drivers' undoubted talent. Ascari did a lap of 4'40.5sec at an average of 173.159km/h (108.224mph), beating the old lap record set by a Jaguar XK120 the year before of 169.356km/h (105.847mph). This car competed in the Mille Miglia of 1952 in the hands of Giovanni Bracco.

1953

Four Ferraris start, one finishes

Jaguar's year again, despite an impressive Ferrari official entry with Alberto Ascari. When Moss retired, having had trouble with his Jaguar, Rolt and Hamilton went into first place and held it, thus giving the Coventry marque its second Le Mans victory.

The winning Jaguar of Rolt and Hamilton covered 4088.064km (2540.205 miles) at an average 170.336km/h (105.842mph).

Ferrari no. 15. Type 340 MM (chassis no. 0320), entered by Scuderia Ferrari, driven by Marzotto and Marzotto. It was fifth in the distance result, covering 3956.660km (2458.555 miles) in 24 hours at an average 164.861km/h (102.440mph).

The brothers Paolo and Gianni achieved the best score of the four Ferraris taking part on the Sarthe circuit this year. Once again a sensible race paid off. In addition this 340 MM came ninth in the Index of Performance. In 11th place in the first hour and seventh in the second, the two Italians gained a shrewd two places to finish fifth behind three Jaguars and a Cunningham.

19

Ferrari no. 16. Type 340 MM (chassis no. 0284), entered by Luigi Chinetti, driven by Cole and Chinetti. It retired in the 16th hour, after being sixth in the preceding hour.

It was at 6.14am that the accident happened on the Maison-Blanche bend. The blue Vignale-bodied roadster left the track at speed and Cole was fatally injured. He was competing in his fourth Le Mans. Number 16 had been third in the overall classification in the second and third hours of the event.

Ferrari no. 12. Type 340 MM (chassis no. 0318), entered by Scuderia Ferrari, driven by Ascari and Villoresi. It retired in the 20th hour, after being eighth during the preceding hour.

This Ferrari was fitted with the 'big' 4.5-litre engine developed for Indianapolis the previous year. With two particularly fast drivers at the wheel, this 340 MM was involved in the tussle at the front and even led the event for a time (in the seventh hour), taking the lap record at 181.642km/h (112.867mph). Unfortunately the car's clutch could not take the extra power of the new engine, nor the hell-for-leather pace set from the start of the event. This Ferrari retired at 10.59am on the Mulsanne bend.

Ferrari no. 14. Type 340 MM (chassis no. 0322), entered by Scuderia Ferrari, driven by Farina and Hawthorn. It went out in the second hour, after being in 47th position in the first hour.

Ferrari number 14 was put out of the event at 5.05pm for having its brake fluid replenished within 28 laps. In fact the mechanics had forgotten the 28 laps rule between each refuelling, which also applied to brake fluid.

1954

Four Ferraris start, one finishes

A second Ferrari victory at Le Mans. This year's Le Mans 24 Hours, which took place in torrential rain, saw yet another Ferrari–Jaguar duel: this time it went in favour of the former. A Gordini driven by Simon and Behra seemed at times to be fiercely in contention, but ignition problems pushed it back.

Ferrari no. 4. Type 375-plus, Sports (chassis no. 0396), registration no. Prova MO 36, entered by Scuderia Ferrari, driven by Gonzales and Trintignant. It came first on distance, covering 4061.150km (2523.482 miles) in 24 hours at an average 169.215km/h (105.145mph). The sole surviving Ferrari only attained its goal by a small margin, giving the Maranello firm its second Le Mans victory.
The Ferrari defended its leading position, keeping a little under 5km (3 miles) between it and the Jaguar of Rolt and Hamilton after 24 hours of driving in very unpleasant weather. Besides its distance win, the 375-plus number 4 was first in the Index of Performance, and the Argentinian Froilan Gonzales was rewarded with the fastest lap: 4' 16.8sec at 189.139km/h (117.526mph).

Ferrari no. 5. Type 375-plus, Sports (chassis no. 0392), driven by L. Rosier and Manzon. It retired in the 15th hour, after being in third place in the previous hour.
Fifth in the first and second hours, the Ferrari of these two French drivers had a remarkable race, even occupying second position for three hours. The struggle with the Jaguars strained the gearbox, which refused to finish a race that had been so well executed.

Ferrari no. 6. Type C 375 MM, Sports (chassis no. 0372 AM; registration no. 6D 11 43), entered by B. Cunningham, driven by Walters and Fitch. It retired in the 13th hour, after being in 20th place in the preceding hour.
It was Briggs Cunningham who modified this Ferrari 375 MM and put it into the 1954 24 Hours to run in his colours. The geat technical innovation in this American Ferrari lay in its system of water-cooled hydraulic brakes. The bodywork, too, was adapted to American taste. After three hours in which it was very creditably placed (seventh and sixth), the Cunningham Ferrari dropped to the lower rankings before withdrawing with rear-axle problems.

Ferrari no. 3. Type 375-plus, Sports (chassis no. 0394), entered by Scuderia Ferrari, driven by Maglioli and P. Marzotto. It retired in the eighth hour, after being second in the preceding hour.

This official Ferrari was in the leading group until its withdrawal with gearbox trouble; it was in second place in the general classification in all the hours it ran except for the fifth, when it was lying in third. This Italian team had the benefit of the Ferrari 375-plus that had previously been victorious at Silverstone in the expert hands of Gonzales.

Ferrari no. 18. Type 375 MM, Sports (chassis no. 0380; registration no. 35277 BO), entered by Luigi Chinetti, driven by Rubirosa and Biaggio. It retired in the second hour, after being 52nd in the first hour.

Count Biaggio went wide coming out of the Mulsanne, ending up in the sand. This very pretty Berlinetta, which had been exhibited at the Geneva Salon in March 1954, did not get far, despite the labours of its distinguished driver-turned-navvy.

1955

Five Ferraris start, none finish

This year was the return of Mercedes, hoping to challenge the Jaguars and Ferraris on territory they knew well. Tragically, a happy occasion became a hideous nightmare when at 6.28 in the evening the remains of Pierre Levegh's Mercedes hurtled into the crowd, killing 81 people.

The winners were the team of Hawthorn and Bueb in a Jaguar D with an average of 172.308km/h (107.067mph) over 4135.380km (2569.606 miles).

Ferrari no. 5. Type 735 LM (chassis no. 0546; registration no. MO 49), entered by Scuderia Ferrari, driven by Trintignant and Schell. It retired in the 10th hour, after being 10th in the preceding hour.

After quite a bad start this team climbed from 54th to 10th before pulling out with an overheated engine.

Ferrari no. 12. Type 750 M, Sports (chassis no. 0440), entered by 'Heldé', driven by Lucas and 'Heldé'. It retired in the 10th hour, after being in 18th place in the preceding hour.

The distributor let down these Le Mans regulars.

Ferrari no. 4. Type 735 LM (chassis no. 0532; registration no. MO 36), entered by Scuderia Ferrari, driven by Castellotti and Marzotto. It retired in the fifth hour, after lying seventh in the preceding hour.

The start of the event saw a free-for-all between Fangio's Mercedes, Hawthorn's Jaguar and this Ferrari driven by Castellotti. These three Formula 1 drivers contended fiercely, succeeding one another at the top of the general classification. Unfortunately the Ferrari's engine, of which so much was demanded, gave up the ghost early on, although Castellotti was in the lead at the end of the first hour.

Ferrari no. 3. Type 735 LM, Sports (chassis no. 0558; registration no. MO 31), entered by Scuderia Ferrari, driven by Maglioli and P. Hill. It retired in the seventh hour, after being 10th in the preceding hour.

A punctured radiator caused a loss of time, then the clutch packed up, forcing this Ferrari to withdraw after a brilliant start: fourth during the first three hours, then third.

Ferrari no. 14. Type 750 M, Sports (chassis no. 0504), entered by Sparken, driven by Sparken and Gregory. It retired in the third hour, after being in 27th place in the preceding hour.

This was the first Ferrari to withdraw.

1956

Six Ferraris start, one finishes

After the disaster of the previous year the circuit was considerably modified, notably with regard to the realignment of the stands, which were redesigned to prevent any future catastrophes.

After the early laps two Jaguar Ds and a Ferrari were eliminated by a minor collision, which removed some of the interest from the event.

The winners of the event were Sanderton and Flockhart in a Jaguar D at an average of 168.122km/h (104.466mph) over 4034.929km (2507.189 miles).

Ferrari no. 12. Type 625 LM, Sports (chassis no. 0644; registration no. 36 MO), entered by Scuderia Ferrari, driven by Gendebien and Trintignant. Third in the distance classification, it covered 3937.611km (2446.718 miles) at an average 164.067km/h (101.947mph).
This was the sole surviving Ferrari from the 1955 Le Mans, and finished in third place behind the Jaguar D of the winners and the Aston Martin DB 3S which came second.
It was due to a very intelligent race that this Belgian-French team improved from sixth place in the first hour to third at the finish (and seventh in the Index of Performance). They made the best possible use of the 225bhp of their 2.5-litre engine in their battle with the 3.4 litres and 3 litres of the Jaguar and Aston Martin respectively.

Ferrari no. 22. Type 500 TR, Sports (chassis no. 0654; registration no.66943 BO), entered by the 'Los Amigos' group, driven by Picard and Tappan. It retired in the 14th hour, after being 11th in the previous hour.
This blue and white Ferrari was disqualified when it was leading the 2-litre class. It ran out of fuel 32 laps after refuelling (the rules demand a minimum 34 laps between each refuelling) and was refuelled anyway.

Ferrari no. 10. Type 625 LM, Sports (chassis no. 0632; registration no. 31 MO), entered by Scuderia Ferrari, driven by Simon and P. Hill. It retired in the 10th hour, after being fourth in the ninth hour.
This very fast team moved between fourth and fifth position before being let down by the transmission.

Ferrari no. 20. Type 500 TR, Sports (chassis no. 0618; registration no. 63281 BO), entered by the Belgian national team, driven by L. Bianchi and de Changy. It retired in the eighth hour, after being in 13th place in the preceding hour.
The Belgians led the 2-litre class for some time, despite a few scares on the Mulsanne bend. It was there, too, that they finished with a broken distributor.

Ferrari no. 21. Type 500 TR, Sports (chassis no. 0624), entered by Pierre Meyrat, driven by Tavano and Meyrat. It retired in the eighth hour, after being 30th in the preceding hour.

The atmosphere was highly charged when, at 10pm, the public saw smoke rising from the track a little way in front of the stands. For an instant the memory of the frightful incident the year before hovered over Le Mans. Glöckler's Porsche had been in collision with this Ferrari. The two cars spun round and Tavano was flung out with a broken nose; the Porsche was destroyed by fire after its driver had got out with burns and a broken leg.

Ferrari no. 11. Type 625 LM, Sports, entered by Scuderia Ferrari, driven by de Portago and Hamilton. It retired in the first hour.

The Marquis de Portago took the start. The contest in the leading group was intense. On the second lap Paul Frère and Jack Fairman in Jaguar Ds collided on the Tertre-Rouge S-bends. De Portago arrived just as Fairman was trying to start up again. The impact was not very violent, but it was enough to put out the 625 LM.

1957

Nine Ferraris start, two finish

Five Jaguars in the first six places – Ferrari was defeated by a knockout! The British firm was officially absent from the event, but the privateers (or semi-officials) were very much there to give the Coventry company its fifth (and third consecutive) win.

The winners of the event, Flockhart and Bueb, in a Jaguar D, took it with an average of 183.213km/h (113.843mph) over 4397.108km (2732.236 miles).

Ferrari no. 8. Type 315 S, Sports (chassis no. 0684), entered by Scuderia Ferrari, driven by Lewis Evans and Severi. It came fifth on distance, covering 4031.618km (2505.131 miles) at an average of 197.984km/h (123.026mph).

The Briton Lewis Evans, a newcomer to the Ferrari team, was partnered with the mechanic-fitter Martino Severi. It was the first of the Ferraris to finish, and the only 12-cylinder model. It was by some most intelligent driving that this mixed team held on to its fifth place from 10pm on Saturday to 4pm on Sunday.

Twenty minutes or so from the end the Ferrari made a stop at the pits and for a moment it seemed as if Hamilton's Jaguar would snatch the fifth spot, but luckily they held him off (this would have put five Jaguar Ds in the first five places).

Ferrari no. 28. Type 500 TRC, Sports (chassis no. 0682), entered by the Belgian national team, driven by L. Bianchi and Harris. It was seventh on distance, covering 3869.080km (2404.135 miles) at an average 161.212km/h (100.172mph).

This 2-litre won its class (1501–2000cc) after a very consistent drive that took it from 21st to seventh in the general classification.

Ferrari no. 27. Type 500 TRC, Sports (chassis no. 0696), entered by F. Tavano, driven by Tavano and Péron. It retired in the 23rd hour, after lying in 14th place, when engine failure put a stop to this local French Ferrari.

Ferrari no. 10. Type 290 MM, Sports (chassis no. 0616), entered by Luigi Chinetti, driven by Arents and de Vroom. it retired in the 16th hour, after being in seventh place in the preceding hour.
A problem with the brakes forced this American Ferrari to withdraw after a spectacular recovery from 18th place in the first hour to seventh before its retirement.

Ferrari no. 29. Type 500 TRC, Sports (chassis no. 0706), entered by 'Los Amigos' and F. Picard, driven by Picard and Ginther. It retired in the 14th hour, after being in 18th place in the preceding hour.
A defective water pump immobilized this Ferrari which gave the American Richie Ginther his first Le Mans drive.

Ferrari no. 9. Type 250 TR, Sports (chassis no. 0526), entered by Scuderia Ferrari, driven by Gendebien and Trintignant. It retired in the 10th hour, after lying in 11th place the previous hour.

Before the start of the event all eyes were on this new machine, based on the brilliant Testa Rossa and fitted with the same 12-cylinder unit as the GT car used by Gendebien in the Mille Miglia. After making a very fast start the Franco-Belgian team retired just after midnight with piston trouble (some of the other Ferraris went out with the same problem). The highest speed clocked by this machine on the Hunaudières was 244.068km/h (151.657mph).

Ferrari no. 6. Type 335 C, Sports (chassis no. 0700), entered by Scuderia Ferrari, driven by P. Hill and Collins. It retired officially in the second hour. At the start, however, Peter Collins had been the fastest into his car and had set off in this Ferrari, which he knew well, having driven it in the Mille Miglia and at the Nürburgring. Unfortunately Collins was already having engine trouble on the second lap and was lying 10th. On the next lap he stopped and the incredulous mechanics diagnosed a cracked piston. Three good laps and that was it.

Ferrari no. 11. Type 290 MM, sports (chassis no. 0606), entered by the Belgian national team, driven by Swaters and de Changy. It retired in the ninth hour after being in 36th place the previous hour.

Once again it was a piston that caused the retirement of this Belgian Ferrari, although it had never been brilliantly placed.

33

Ferrari no. 61. Type 500 TRC, Sports (chassis no. 0686), entered by Gotfrid Köchert, driven by Köchert and Bauer. It retired in the third hour, after lying in 47th position.
This was a reserve car but was nevertheless able to start as it benefited from a last-minute withdrawal. A carburation problem forced this Austrian Ferrari to withdraw.

Ferrari no. 7. Type 335 S, Sports (chassis no. 0656), entered by Scuderia Ferrari, driven by Hawthorn and Musson. It retired in the fifth hour, after being in fourth place the previous hour.
With the Collins Ferrari eliminated after the early laps, it was Mike Hawthorn who took the lead and imposed a pace worthy of the Grands Prix the perpetually bow-tied Englishman knew so well. He was doing so well that he beat the lap record with a time of 3'58.7sec, an average of 203.015km/h (126.148mph). Thus he crossed the 200km/h (124mph) threshold and smashed the former record set the previous year in a Jaguar D – driven by Mike Hawthorn (4'20sec lap; 186.383km/h or 115.813mph). The Ferrari clocked a maximum speed of 289.550km/h (179.918mph). Unfortunately Luigi Musso retired a few hours later, nursing his 335 S along the Hunaudières with, like Collins, a cracked piston.

1958

Ten Ferraris start, three finish

The third victory at the Le mans 24 Hours for Ferrari, who were challenging Aston Martin and, in particular, Jaguar, who were seeking a sixth outright win. In fact the great duel did not take place and the Le Mans spectators were amazed to see the little Porsches turn in a superb performance, placing their 1600cc car in third position, behind the Ferrari and the 3-litre Aston Martin.

Ferrari no. 14. Type 250 TR, Sports (chassis no. 0728), entered by Scuderia Ferrari, driven by Gendebien and P. Hill. It came first on distance, covering 4101.926km (2548.819 miles) at an average 170.914km/h (106.201mph).
The Ferrari victory the Le Mans crowd witnessed this year, the company's third, was a very fraught one. From the third hour out the American-Belgian team took the lead and held it to the finish. Because of the severe weather conditions this Ferrari covered a distance 295km (183 miles) less than that of the winning Jaguar the previous year.

Ferrari no. 21. Type 250 TR, Sports (chassis no. 0736; registration no. BO 98194), entered by the Belgian national team, driven by 'Beurlys' and de Changy. It was sixth on distance, covering 3744.613km (2326.795 miles) at an average 156.026km/h (96.950mph).

A very modest average speed for this second Ferrari to finish, but it was the result of the weather and of a considerable delay incurred during the evening. The Belgians came 14th in the Index of Performance.

Ferrari no. 22. Type 250 TR, Sports (chassis no. 0732), entered by Hugus, driven by Hugus and Eriksson. It was placed seventh on distance, having covered 3733.043km (2319.605 miles) at an average 155.543km/h (96.650mph).

This blue and white American Ferrari was the third and last to finish, at such a low average speed that it would have been in 11th position the previous year. Unfortunately the conditions were appalling and the cause of numerous accidents.

Ferrari no. 25. Type 250 TR, Sports (chassis no. 0600), entered by Luigi Chinetti-North American Racing Team, driven by P. Rodriguez and José Behra. It retired in the 14th hour, after being in 14th place in the preceding hour.

Ricardo Rodriguez should have partnered his brother Pedro at the wheel of this NART Ferrari. Unfortunately only the elder, Pedro (18 years old), was able to line up at the start, leaving his 16-year-old brother behind. It was José, Jean Behra's brother, who took his place, but the event ended for them with a water radiator damaged by severe overheating.

Ferrari no. 12. Type 250 TR, Sports (chassis no. 0704), entered by Scuderia Ferrari, driven by Hawthorn and Collins. It retired with clutch trouble in the 11th hour, after being in ninth place the previous hour.

Ferrari no. 16. Type 250 TR, Sports (chassis no. 0726; registration no. 99785 BO), driven by Von Trips and Seidel. It retired in the ninth hour, after being in third place in the preceding hour.

This team of German drivers made a very good start, staying in the front squad consistently. As the hours passed they competed on equal terms with the best, varying between third and fourth place. Unfortunately Wolfgang Seidel left the road at a quarter past midnight at Arnage. The car ended up stuck in the mud, from which Seidel was unable to extricate it.

Ferrari no. 19. Type 250 TR, Sports (chassis no. 0730), driven by Martin and Tavano. It retired in the eighth hour, after being in 13th place in the preceding hour.

Two reasons accounted for its withdrawal: a defective ignition and a worn out clutch.

Ferrari no. 17. Type 250 TR, Sports (chassis no. 0722), entered by Fernand Tavano, driven by Gomez Mena and Drogo. It retired in the seventh hour after being 39th in the preceding hour: it went out with engine failure near the Mulsanne.

Ferrari no. 18. Type 250 TR, Sports (chassis no. 0756), entered by North American Racing Team, driven by Gurney and Kessler. It retired in the seventh hour, after being 17th the previous hour.
The American Bruce Kessler was at the wheel when the car collided with the Jaguar D of 'Mary', alias Brousselet, who was killed. The Ferrari caught fire and was completely destroyed. Kessler was taken to hospital with multiple bruising.

Ferrari no. 20. Type 250 TR, Sports (chassis no. 0748), entered by François Picard, driven by Picard and Juhan. It retired in the seventh hour, after being in 10th place in the preceding hour.
The conditions in which this event was run were so bad that several cars did not see the inadequately marked wreckage of a Lotus. Picard's Ferrari was unable to avoid it, rammed it and finished its race under the famous Dunlop footbridge. Damage to the Ferrari was too extensive for any hope of restarting. Happily, the French driver was only slightly injured.

Ferrari no. 58. Type 250 TR, Sports (chassis no. 0724), entered by the Belgian national team, driven by L. Bianchi and Mairesse. It retired after an accident in the fourth hour, after being in 23rd position in the third hour.

1959

Eleven Ferraris start, four finish

A good close grouping of GT Ferraris, which placed themselves third, fourth, fifth and sixth in the general classification, certainly dominated this category. None of the powerful Ferrari 250 Testa Rossas finished in an event that bore the masterly stamp of the Aston Martin team.

The winners of the event were Salvadori and Shelby in an Aston Martin DBR1, at an average speed of 181.163km/h (112.569mph) over 4347.900km (2701.660 miles).

Ferrari no. 11. Type 250 GT, GT category (chassis no. 1321 GT), entered by Ecurie Francorchamps, driven by 'Heldé' and Beurlys. It came third on distance, having covered 4001.601km (2486.480 miles) at 166.733km/h (103.603mph).

This was the first Ferrari to be placed, at some 350km (218 miles) behind the winners. For this GT car third place overall was a first-rate performance as it put it not far behind the two Aston Martin Sports.

Ferrari no. 18. Type 250 GT, GT category (chassis no. 1461 GT), entered by North American Racing Team, driven by A. Pillette and Arents. It came fourth on distance, covering 3991.447km (2480.170 miles) at an average 166.310km/h (103.340mph).

This car marked the first appearance of a Scaglietti body on a Ferrari GT. Its result was balanced by a second placing in the GT category.

Ferrari no. 16. Type 250 GT California Spyder, GT category (chassis no. 1451 GT), entered by Fernand Tavano, driven by Tavano and Grossman. It was placed fifth on distance, covering 3964.491km (2463.421 miles) at an average 165.187km/h (102.642mph).

This was the first appearance of a 250 GT Spyder at the Le Mans 24 Hours and, what is more, it was very creditably placed at the end of the two times round the clock.

Ferrari no. 20. Type 250 GT, category GT (chassis no. 1377 GT), driven by Fayen and Munaron. It finished sixth on distance, covering 3954.691km (2457.331 miles) at an average 164.779km/h (102.389mph).

Like Pillette's car, this Ferrari wore Scaglietti bodywork.

Ferrari no. 14. Type 250 TR, Sports (chassis no. 0766), entered by Scuderia Ferrari, driven by Gendebien and P. Hill. It retired in the 20th hour, after being in first place the previous hour.

This was Scuderia's 'sensible' partnership. The two drivers stuck scrupulously to their schedule and seemed not to be interested in the tussle going on at the top of their group. Their steady persistence almost paid off as they took over the lead from the 11th hour, before an overheated engine forced their withdrawal.

Ferrari no. 12. Type 250 TR, Sports (chassis no. 0774), entered by Scuderia Ferrari, driven by Behra and Gurney. It retired in the 10th hour, after being in fourth place in the preceding hour.

Third in the first hour, then in the lead from the second to the sixth hours, this Ferrari lost one place per hour until its retirement. This car was in the forefront of the skirmishing with Moss's Aston Martin, which itself acted as the 'hare' to take the wind out of the Italian machines.

Ferrari no. 19. Type 250 TR, Sports (chassis no. 0730), entered by E. D. Martin, driven by Martin and Kimberly. It retired in the eighth hour, after being in ninth place in the preceding hour.

The transmission let this Ferrari down; ninth had been its best placing.

Ferrari no. 23. Type Dino, Sports, driven by Cabianca and Scarlatti. It retired with a carburation problem in the sixth hour, after being in 21st position the previous hour.

Ferrari no. 10. Type 250 TR, Sports (chassis no. 0736), entered by the Belgian national team, driven by L. Bianchi and de Changy. It retired in the fifth hour with fuel-feed trouble, after being 25th in the preceding hour.
This Belgian Ferrari would have occupied 12th place in the general classification.

Ferrari no. 15. Type 250 TR, Sports (chassis no. 0770), entered by Scuderia Ferrari, driven by Allison and Da Silva Ramos. It retired in the fourth hour, after being in seventh position in the third hour.
Another Ferrari that was too closely involved in the tussle at the front. After being in fourth place for a while, it had to give up with a wrecked gearbox.

Ferrari no. 17. Type 250 TR, Sports (chassis no. 0666), entered by North American Racing Team, driven by Carveth and Geithner. It retired in the third hour after being in 40th place in the second hour before it went out with a shattered gearbox.

1960

Twelve Ferraris start, six finish

A fourth victory in the Le Mans 24 Hours for Ferrari, all the more brilliant in that it was the Testa Rossas that carried off the first two positions; the Maranello firm put six cars in the first seven places. The only stranger in this tight grouping was the Aston Martin of Clark and Salvadori.

Ferrari no. 11. Type TR 60, Sports (chassis no. 0772), entered by Scuderia Ferrari, driven by Gendebien and Frère. It won, covering 4217.527km (2620.650 miles) at an average 175.730km/h (109.194mph).
Ferrari's shrewdness paid off. In a second edition of the 1959 event Gendebien, partnering Paul Frère this time, pressed on to the end and carried off a fine victory and a second place in the Index of Performance. Second at the end of the first hour, Genedebien and Frère then held the lead to the final hour. There is some debate about the chassis number of this car, which Ginther is supposed to have destroyed in the Targa Florio.

Ferrari no. 17. Type 250 TR, Sports (chassis no. 0766), entered by North American Racing Team, driven by A. Pillette and R. Rodriguez. It came second on distance, covering 4163.666km (2587.182 miles) at an average 173.486km/h (107.799mph). A fantastic début for the 17-year-old Ricardo Rodriquez who held off another youngster – Jim Clark in an Aston Martin.

Ferrari no. 18. Type 250 GT, category GT (chassis no. 1931 GT; registration no. EE 02015), entered by North American Racing Team, driven by Arents and Connell. It was fifth on distance, covering 4030.271km (2504.294 miles) at an average 167.928km/h (104.346mph). This 250 GT clocked a 4′14.5sec lap.

Ferrari no. 16. Type 250 GT, category GT (chassis no. 2001 GT), entered by Fernand Tavano, driven by Tavano and 'Loustel'. It came fourth on distance, covering 4055.928km (2520.237 miles) at an average 168.997km/h (105.010mph).

Tavano and Pierre 'Loustel', alias Pierre Dumay, were lying ninth in the first hour. After a splendid race they took the GT class.

Ferrari no. 22. Type 250 GT, category GT (chassis no. 2021 GT; registration no. MO 57808), entered by Ecurie Francorchamps, driven by Noblet and 'Eldé'. It was sixth on distance, covering 4029.004km (2503.507 miles) at an average 167.875km/h (104.313mph).

Ferrari no. 19. Type 250 GT, category GT (chassis no. 1759 GT; registration no. 02016 EE), entered by North American Racing Team, driven by Hugus and Pabst. It came seventh, covering 4019.930km (2497.869 miles) at an average 167.497km/h (104.078mph).

Ferrari no. 20. Type 250 GT, category GT (chassis no. 2015 GT; registration no. 02014), entered by North American Racing Team, driven by Sturgis and Schlesser. It retired in the 22nd hour, after being in 11th position the preceding hour.

Ferrari no. 15. Type 250 GT, category GT (chassis no. 2009 GT), entered by G. Whitehead, driven by Whitehead and Taylor. It retired in the 21st hour, after being in fifth position after 20 hours, leaving Tavano to win the GT class.

Ferrari no. 10. Type TR 60, Sports (chassis no. 0770), entered by Scuderia Ferrari, driven by Mairesse and Ginther. It retired in the 17th hour with a damaged gearbox, after being in third place in the preceding hour. This official Ferrari was in second place in the general class for a long period.

Ferrari no. 21. Type 250 GT, category GT (chassis no. 1811 GT; registration no. 02010 EE), entered by the Belgian national team, driven by 'Beurlys' and L. Bianchi. It retired dramatically after three hours, having been in 12th place.

Ferrari no. 12. Type TRI/60, Sports (chassis no. 0782), entered by Scuderia Ferrari, driven by Scarfiotti and P. Rodriguez. It retired in the third hour, after being 33rd the preceding hour.

The original intention was for this car to be driven by the two brothers Pedro and Ricardo Rodriguez, with Lodovico Scarfiotti as reserve driver. In the end Ricardo drove number 17 with Pillette, leaving his brother with Scarfiotti and misfortune. Pedro ran out of fuel on the circuit and, furious, returned on foot. He shouted to the mechanics 'If you didn't have enough gas you should have made it up with water!'

Ferrari no. 9. Type TRI/60, Sports (chassis no. 0780), entered by Scuderia Ferrari, driven by P. Hill and Von Trips. It retired in the third hour after being in 32nd position.

This car was originally intended for Gendebien and Phil Hill, but these two were split up – for the better fortune of Gendebien. It was the silliest of errors – an empty tank – that prevented Hill and Von Trips from pursuing their luck to the end.

Ferrari no. 14. Type 250 GT, category GT (chassis no. 1999 GT), entered by Scuderia Serenissima, driven by Abate and Balzarini. Damaged in a mishap in practice, this 250 GT did not take part in the event – you can see why.

1961

Eleven Ferraris start, four finish

The fifth victory at the Le Mans 24 Hours for Ferrari, who put three cars in the first three places in the event and also carried off the GT class. Phil Hill scored his second win and Olivier Gendebien his third; these two drivers were hardly strangers to the Le Mans crowd.

Ferrari no. 10. Type 250 TRI/61, Sports (chassis no. 0780), entered by SEFAC-Ferrari, driven by Gendebien and P. Hill. It was first on distance, covering 4476.580km (2781.618 miles) at an average 186.524km/h (115.901mph).
Aftering standing up well to the Mexican fury, and watched by Signora Ferrari, representing her husband at Le Mans, Gendebien and Hill won a thrilling event, fully in keeping with the glory of Ferrari today.

Ferrari no. 11. Type 250 TRI/61, Sports, entered by SEFAC-Ferrari, driven by Mairesse and Parkes. It was second on distance, covering 4438.718km (2758.092 miles) at an average 184.947km/h (114.921mph).

The retirement of the Rodriguez brothers and of Ginther and Von Trips benefited Mairesse and Parkes, who achieved a really consistent performance.

Ferrari no. 14. Type 250 GT, category GT (chassis no. 2689 GT), entered by Pierre Noblet, driven by Noblet and Guichet. It came third on distance, covering 4258.009km (2546.804 miles) at an average 177.417km/h (110.242mph).

This car won the GT category, achieving 40km (25 miles) more in the 24 hours than the overall winners, Frère and Gendebien, the previous year.

Ferrari no. 20. Type 250 GT, category GT (chassis no. 2731 GT; registration no. 06150 L4), entered by the Belgian national team, driven by Grossman and A. Pillette. It was sixth on distance, covering 4150.302km (2578.878 miles) at an average 172.929km/h (107.453mph).

Ferrari no. 17. Type 250 TR/I/61, Sports (registration no. 06183 L4 and Prova MO 31), entered by North American Racing Team, driven by Pedro and Ricardo Rodriguez. It retired in the 23rd hour, after being second the previous hour.

The two fiery Mexicans came close to beating the all-powerful Scuderia Ferrari in their private entry. In the course of this one event these two very young men became the heroes of a generation of spectators. They were often in the lead, at the risk of running out fuel, with a worst placing of fourth. Close to the finish their engine gave up the ghost and, to an ovation from the crowd, Ferrari number 17 was pushed back to the pits by the mechanics. Ricardo set the lap record at 3′59.09sec, or 201.202km/h (125.021mph).

Ferrari no. 23. Type 246 SP, Sports (chassis no. 0796), entered by SEFAC-Ferrari, driven by Ginther and Von Trips. It retired in the 17th hour after being second the previous hour.

Another leading Ferrari that had to retire with an empty tank.

Ferrari no. 12. Type 250 GT Experimental, category GT (chassis no. 2643 GT; registration no. 06233 L4 and Prova MO 53), entered by SEFAC-Ferrari, driven by Tavano and Baghetti. It retired in the 13th hour, after lying eighth in the preceding hour.

This historic car was actually the prototype of the future GTO, with a body by Pininfarina on a short-chassis 250 GT fitted with a Testa Rossa engine. Despite some aerodynamic problems, and a serious one with the engine which forced its retirement, this car displayed amazing potential.

Ferrari no. 16. Type 250 GT, category GT (chassis no. 2733 GT; registration no. MO 6626), entered by Scuderia Serenissima, driven by Trintignant and Abate. It retired in the third hour, after being in 12th place during the preceding hour.

Minor troubles (a jammed throttle linkage) preceded a bigger problem that could not be put right: a broken axle.

Ferrari no. 18. Type 250 GT, category GT (chassis no. 2735 GT; registration no. 66178 MO), entered by North American Racing Team, but wearing the colours of Rob Walkers, driven by Moss and G. Hill. It retired in the 10th hour, after being in sixth place in the ninth hour.

At 1.35am this 250 GT came to a final stop with a broken radiator hose. The retirement of the star team revived the hopes of the Frenchmen Noblet and Guichet, who saw the prospect of a GT victory appear over the horizon. Earlier the rejoicing spectators had seen the little GT outrun Mairesse's Sports machine.

Ferrari no. 15. Type 250 GT, category GT (chassis no. 2129 GT; registration no. MO 59763), entered by Ecurie Francorchamps, driven by Berger and L. Bianchi. It retired in the seventh hour, after being in 40th place the preceding hour.

This Belgian car was the first of the Ferrari retirements.

Ferrari no. 57. Type 250 GT, category GT (chassis no. 2729 GT; registration no. 66193 MO), entered by Roger de Lageneste, driven by Lageneste and Dumay.

This car, although entered, did not start.

Ferrari no. 19. Type 250 GT, category GT (chassis no. 2725 GT; registration no. 06149 L4), entered by North American Racing Team, driven by Reed and Arents. It retired in the seventh hour with a short circuit, after being 13th.

1962

Fifteen Ferraris start, five finish

The sixth victory for Ferrari on this circuit that Scuderia knew so well. A third victory came for Phil Hill, and Gendebien completed his brilliant tally of four Le Mans wins.

From the start the new Ferrari GTO showed its fantastic potential, writing a page of history when it finished second in the general classification.

Ferrari no. 6. Type 330 LM, Experimental (chassis no. 0808), entered by SEFAC-Ferrari, driven by P. Hill and Gendebien. It was first on distance, covering 4451.255km (2765.882 miles) at an average 185.469km/h (115.245 mph).

This was the fourth victory at Le Mans for Olivier Genedebien, the third for Phil Hill and the sixth for the Ferrari marque, which was building its reputation on the circuit. This win by the only survivor of the Scuderia Ferrari established the 4-litre power unit and, historically, it was the last front-engined Ferrari to take the 24-hour event. The winners' 350 LM took the lead on the second lap and did not relinquish it until the end. Phil Hill had the satisfaction of setting the lap and circuit record at 3'57.3sec, or 204.202km/h, breaking the former record of 3'58.7sec set in 1957 by Mike Hawthorn in a Ferrari 412.

Ferrari no. 19. Type 250 GTO, category GT (chassis no. 3705 GT), entered by Pierre Noblet, driven by Guichet and Noblet. It came second on distance, covering 4384.135km (2724.175 miles) at an average 182.673km/h (113.077mph).

The north and south of France were in partnership once again for the greater glory of Ferrari and the GTO. Pierre Noblet from Roubaix and Jean Guichet from Marseilles accomplished a drive of remarkable consistency and speed. The two drivers, who had been victorious in GTs the previous year in an SWB, earned second place after holding this position from the 17th hour to the end. In addition this GTO won the 2501–3000cc class.

Ferrari no. 22. Type 250 GTO, category GT (chassis no. 3757), entered by the Belgian national team, driven by 'Eldé' and 'Beurlys'. It came third, covering 4213.875km (2618.380 miles) at an average 175.578km/h (109.099mph).
The rout of the official Ferraris (except number 6) benefited the Belgian GTO managed by Jacques Swaters. It came second in the GT class, a little more than 100km (62 miles) behind the winners in this category.

Ferrari no. 17. Type 250 GTO, Experimental (chassis no. 3223 GT; registration no. 28790 NY State USA), entered by North American Racing Team, driven by Grossman and Roberts. It was sixth on distance, covering 3997.810km (2484.124 miles) at an average 166.575km/h (103.505mph).

Ferrari no. 21. Type 250 GT Experimental, category GT (chassis no. 2643 GT), entered by W. S. McKelvey, driven by Hugus and Reed. It was ninth on distance, covering 3779.317km (2348.359 miles) at an average 157.472km/h (97.849mph).

Third and last Ferrari GT, this car had already been seen the year before wearing number 12. The Americans had the merit of finishing.

Ferrari no. 27. Type 268 SP, Experimental (chassis no. 0798), entered by SEFAC-Ferrari, driven by Baghetti and Scarfiotti. It retired in the 18th hour, after being third in the preceding hour.

The gearbox brought about the retirement of this second mid-engined Ferrari.

Ferrari no. 23. Type 250 GTO, category GT (chassis no. 3769 GT), entered by Fernand Tavano, driven by Tavano and Simon. It retired in the 16th hour, after being fifth in the previous hour.

At 7.30 on the Sunday morning André Simon and Fernand Tavano had to relinquish their second place in the GT class and overall, out with a broken axle.

Ferrari no. 18. Type 250 TR/61, Experimental (chassis no. 0794), entered by North American Racing Team, driven by Fulp and Ryan. It retired in the 15th hour, after being in 25th place the preceding hour.

John Fulp and Peter Ryan had to withdraw after their car went into the sand on the Mulsanne bend. This had already happened to them in practice.

Ferrari no. 20. Type 250 GTO, category GT (chassis no. 3505 GT; registration no. 75722 MO), entered by U. D. T. Laystall, driven by Ireland and Gregory. It retired with dynamo trouble in the 15th hour, after being in 13th place.

Ferrari no. 28. Type 246 SP, Experimental (chassis no. 0796), entered by SEFAC-Ferrari, driven by P. Rodriguez and R. Rodriguez. It retired in the 15th hour, after leading in the previous hour.

The Rodriguez brothers were the darlings of Le Mans; every year they provided the spectators with a marvellous spectacle. From the start their little mid-engined Ferrari mixed it with the big Ferraris, and was often in the lead. At 4.45am the gearbox gave up, not up to such rough duelling or such a long straight as the Hunaudières.

Ferrari no. 58. Type 250 GTO, category GT (chassis no. 3445 GT), entered by Scuderia SSS 'Republica di Venezia', driven by Vaccarela and Scarlatti. It retired in the 15th hour with dynamo trouble, after being in 10th place the previous hour.

Ferrari no. 7. Type 330 GT, Experimental (chassis no. 3765), entered by SEFAC-Ferrari, driven by Parkes and Bandini. It retired in the seventh hour, after being in 42nd place in the preceding hour.
Mike Parkes took the wheel at the start in this prototype 330 LM with its GTO body. He drove into the sand at Mulsanne, being obstructed by Graham Hill's Aston Martin. However, this prototype was full of promise. With its 4-litre engine identical to that fitted in the winners' car, this hybrid GTO achieved second-best time in practice.

Ferrari no. 59. Type 250 GT, category GT (chassis no. 2445 GT), entered by the Belgian national team, driven by Berger and Darville. It retired in the fourth hour, after being in 24th place in the third hour. Darville left the road in this short-chassis Berlinetta on the Arnage bend; not a serious accident for the driver, but the car was in no state to continue.

Ferrari no. 16. Type 250 GT 'Bread Van', Experimental (chassis no. 2819 GT), entered by Scuderia SSS 'Republica di Venezia', driven by Abate and Davis. it retired in the fourth hour, after being in 43rd position in the preceding hour.

This car, well known under its 'Bread Van' title, was the result of the re-bodying of a short-chassis Berlinetta carried out by Neri and Bonachini. Unfortunately it was not able to finish the event because of a damaged transmission.

Ferrari no. 15. Type 250 TRI, Experimental (chassis no. 0792), entered by Scuderia SSS 'Republica di Venezia', driven by Bonnier and Gurney. It retired in the fourth hour, after being in 44th position in the preceding hour.

The third car entered for this 24 Hours by Scuderia SSS (Serenissima) and the third to retire, in this case with a damaged transmission. It should be noted that this team were very creditably placed at the end of the first hour.

1963

Eleven Ferraris start, six finish

The seventh victory at the Le Mans 24 Hours for Ferrari, who had six cars in the first six places in the general classification. It was to take another 20 years, to 1983 and Porsche, before it would be possible to witness a greater superiority of one marque over its rivals. This year, too, the genius of the Commendatore was rewarded with the victory of an Italian team in an Italian car.

Ferrari no. 21. Type 250 P, Prototype (chassis no. 0814), entered by SEFAC-Ferrari, driven by Scarfiotti and Bandini. It came first on distance, covering 4561.710km (2834.515 miles) at an average 190.071km/h (118.105mph).
Ferrari's seventh victory at Le Mans, but this time with a 100 per cent Italian team. In addition, this 250 P had a monopoly of firsts: besides its victory in the general classification it took the Index of Performance, the Prototype class, and won its capacity class. Add to these the distance record and you will understand why the drivers were so happy at the finish. Certainly they benefited from the withdrawal of Mairesse and Surtees, but history will only remember the joy of the Italian drivers on the winners' podium.

Ferrari no. 24. Type 250 GTO, category GT (chassis no. 4293 GT), entered by the Belgian national team, driven by 'Beurlys' and Langlois. It was second on distance, covering 4346.320km (2700.678 miles) at an average 181.097km/h (112.528mph).
Second in the general classification, first in the GT class, second in the Index of Performance: Jacques Swaters could be proud of his drivers, and Enzo Ferrari of his GTO, which assured him of another World Championship title.

Ferrari no. 22. Type 250 P, Prototype (chassis no. 0810), entered by SEFAC-Ferrari, driven by Parkes and Maglioli. it was third on distance, covering 4346.200 (2700.604 miles) at an average 181.092km/h (112.525mph).
This Ferrari 250 P, in the Prototype class, was beaten into third place by only 120m (131yd) by a GTO. The Anglo-Italian team, after a good start, spent a lot of time in the pits, but fought back little by little to this well-deserved third place.

Ferrari no. 25. Type 250 GTO, category GT (chassis no. 4153 GT), entered by the Belgian national team, driven by 'Eldé' and Dumay. It came fourth on distance, covering 4332.780km (2692.265 miles) at an average 180.533km/h (112.178mph).

Second in the GT class, this Belgian pair were even lying second in the general classification for a short while on the Sunday afternoon before being overtaken again by their team mates 'Beurlys' and Langlois in number 24.

Ferrari no. 12. Type 330 LM, Prototype (chassis no. 4725), entered by Maranello Concessionaires Ltd. driven by Sears and Salmon. It was fifth on distance, covering 4219.590km (2621.932 miles) at an average 175.816km/h (109.247mph).
At the start there were four Ferraris with 330/4-litre engines. At the finish only the Sears and Salmon car, entered by the British Ferrari importer, was left. The consistency of the Britons paid off, taking them from 17th place at the end of Saturday afternoon to fifth at the finish.

Ferrari no. 26. Type 250 GTO, category GT (chassis no. 4713 GT; registration no. EE O 2166), entered by North American Racing Team, driven by Gregory and Piper. It came sixth on distance covering 4198.140km (2608.603 miles) at an average 174.923km/h (108.692mph).
A slight bump damaged the nose of this GTO and lost the team some precious minutes, then dynamo trouble delayed it further. Nevertheless this car was in third place in the general classification for four hours in succession.

Ferrari no. 23. Type 250 P, Prototype (chassis no. 0812), entered by SEFAC-Ferrari, driven by Surtees and W. Mairesse. It retired in the 19th hour, after being first in the previous hour.

It was John Surtees who set the lap record with 3′53.3sec, or 207.714km/h (129.067mph). The drama came over 18 hours into the event, on the Sunday morning. The 250 P, had been in the lead for some 15 hours and victory laurels seemed to be in the offing. There were two laps between this team and the Ferrari of the eventual winners, then lying second. During over-hasty refuelling petrol was unfortunately spilled over the exhaust pipes – and the subsequent fire took hold while the car was moving. Willy Mairesse came to a rapid halt and leaped from his blazing machine, injuring his right arm, and thus this excellent pair of drivers lost their chance of probable victory.

Ferrari no. 11. Type 330 LM, prototype (chassis no. 4453), entered by North American Racing Team, driven by Gurney and Hall. It retired in the 10th hour, with a damaged transmission, after being third in the ninth hour.

Ferrari no. 9. Type 330 LM, Prototype (chassis no. 4381), entered by Pierre Noblet-SEFAC-Ferrari, driven by Noblet and Guichet. it retired in the eighth hour, after being 26th in the preceding hour.

After its exploits in two successive Le Mans 24 Hours, this French team had the honour of driving a 330 LM 4-litre Ferrari. Unfortunately, a mechanical problem forced them to withdraw during the night.

Ferrari no. 20. Type 250 GTO, category GT (chassis no. 4757 GT), entered by SEFAC-Ferrari, driven by Tavano and Abate. It retired in the ninth hour, after being in 13th position in the preceding hour.

It was Abate who left the road at Maison-Blanche. For the Frenchman Fernand Tavano there was, however, the pleasure of being engaged officially by Scuderia Ferrari and, for a time, spinning along in third place in the Le Mans 24 Hours!

Ferrari no. 10. Type 330 TR, Prototype (chassis no.0808), entered by North American Racing Team, driven by P. Rodriguez and Penske. It retired in the ninth hour, after being third the previous hour.

Pedro Rodriguez and Roger Penske were allocated the Ferrari Testa Rossa that had been victorious the previous year in the hands of Gendebien and Hill. Chassis 0808, the only front-engined prototype in the event, was put out of action by the talented but impetuous Pedro, who left the road at Arnage.

1964

Twelve Ferraris start, seven finish

The eighth Ferrari victory in the Le Mans 24 Hours, but its last by a works car: the ninth was gained by a private team. On this page of history that was being written it was very gratifying for Frenchmen to read that a compatriot was associated with this victory. Unfortunately, the Ferraris were defeated in the GT class by the Cobra of Gurney and Bondurant.

Ferrari no. 20. Type 275 P, Prototype (chassis no. 0816), entered by SEFAC-Ferrari, driven by Guichet and Vaccarella. It came first on distance, covering 4695.310km (2917.530 miles) at an average 195.638km/h (121.564mph).
Another victory for Ferrari, the eighth, a reward this time for Jean Guichet, who was more accustomed to the GT than the Prototype class. As in the year before, the Ferrari's victory on distance was doubled by a win in the Index of Performance. This works Ferrari, which had seventh best time in practice (3'51sec), drove a very consistent race, picking up places due to withdrawals, particularly of Ford.

Ferrari no. 14. Type 330 P, Prototype (chassis no. 0818), entered by Maranello Concessionaires Ltd, driven by Bonnier and G. Hill. It was second on distance, covering 4622.640km (2872.375 miles) at an average 192.610km/h (119.682mph).
Some small faults held back this British-entered Ferrari, which had a very consistant run.

Ferrari no. 19. Type 330 P, Prototype (chassis no. 0822), entered by SEFAC-Ferrari, driven by Bandini and Surtees. It finished third on distance, covering 4530.140km (2814.899 miles) at an average 188.756km (117.288mph).
Surtees achieved the best time in practice with 3′42sec: a time described as 'staggering' by the magazine *Sport-Auto*, as it beat the best of the Fords (Ginther, 3′45.3sec) by a fair amount. Lorenzo Bandini and John Surtees were held back by a carburation problem and so lost two places.

Ferrari no. 24. Type 250 GTO/64, category GT (chassis no. 5575 GT), entered by the Belgian national team, driven by 'Beurlys' and L. Bianchi. It came fifth on distance, covering 4471.400km (2778.399 miles) at an average 186.308km/h (115.766mph).
It was so cold during the night (4°C) that the fuel lines in this GTO iced over (as it did in the Ireland and Maggs GTO). It was beaten in its class by the Cobra of Gurney and Bondurant. The page had finally turned for the GTO.

Ferrari no. 25. Type 250 GTO 63/64, category GT (chassis no. 4399 GT), entered by Maranello Concessionaires Ltd, driven by Ireland and Maggs. It was sixth on distance, covering 4403.620km (2736.283 miles) at an average 183.484km/h (114.012mph).

Ferrari no. 27. Type 250 GTO/64, category GT (chassis no. 5573 GT), entered by Fernand Tavano, driven by Tavano and Grossman. It was ninth on distance, covering 4238.170km (2633.477 miles) at an average 176.590km/h (109.728mph). Its time in practice was 4'04.9sec. Two bent valves, which should have brought a retirement, cost this GTO a lot of time, and in the end it was passed by two Porsche 904s.

Ferrari no. 23. Type 250 LM, Prototype (chassis no. 5843), entered by the Belgian national team, driven by Dumay and Langlois. It came 16th on distance, covering 4009.500km (2491.388 miles) at an average 167.063km/h (103.806mph). Time in practice: 3′56.4sec.
Pierre Dumay took the start and his participation almost came to an end on the first lap. He was following David Piper when the latter dumped a large amount of oil on the track at the Tertre-Rouge bends. Miraculously Dumay managed to stay on the road. Later, troubles with cooling and the clutch held him back. At Maison-Blanche Dumay lost control of the car and more time was needed to repaire it, which explains this slightly misleading 16th place.

Ferrari no. 21. Type 275 P, Prototype (chassis no. 0820), entered by SEFAC-Ferrari, driven by Parkes and Scarfiotti. It retired in the 12th hour, after being in 34th place in the preceding hour.
After turning in a good time in practice (3′49sec), Parkes started in sixth place. Unfortunately, after a few laps disturbing engine noises led to a series of stops. After this the Ferrari was no longer in contention and finally pulled out with oil-pressure trouble.

Ferrari no. 26. Type 250 GTO/64, category GT (chassis no. 5571 GT), entered by North American Racing Team, driven by Hugus and Rosinski. It retired in the ninth hour, after being in 13th place during the preceding hour.

This GTO/64, driven by the American Hugus, broke its transmission while passing the pits. Its broken shaft stuck in the ground, shattering the rear axle and hurling pieces of metal across the track. One fragment even hit a spectator, and Salmon's Aston Martin burst a tyre on the debris.

Ferrari no. 22. Type 275 P, Prototype (chassis no. 0812), entered by SEFAC-Ferrari, driven by Baghetti and Maglioli. It retired in the seventh hour, after being in 38th position.

Giancarlo Baghetti burned out his clutch at the start and took a very long time to complete his first circuit and return to the pits for repair. When he resumed he was in last place. Coming out of the Arnage corner he saw the wreck of Peter Bolton's Cobra in front of him, and went off the road trying to avoid it. (The Cobra had struck and killed two young people who were in this prohibited section of track.)

Ferrari no. 15. Type 330 P, Prototype (chassis no. 0810), entered by North American Racing Team, driven by P. Rodriguez and Hudson. It retired in the fifth hour, after being in fifth position. Time in practice: 3′45.5sec.

True to his reputation, Pedro Rodriguez went off like a rocket, making a remarkable start. His American partner, Skip Hudson, proved slower during his spells at the wheel. In the end a cracked cylinder head brought retirement.

Ferrari no. 58. Type 250 LM, Prototype (chassis no. 5909), entered by North American Racing Team, driven by Piper and Rindt. It retired in the first hour. Time in practice: 3′53.9sec.

After a good start, right behind Rodriguez, David Piper had serious trouble. The oil pressure became too high and burst the oil filter seal spreading the viscous fluid all over the car, even on to the tyres. It was only with great difficulty that Piper managed to come to a stop on the track and then get back to the pits at reduced speed, there to retire.

1965

Eleven Ferraris start, five finish

The ninth Ferrari victory at the Le Mans 24 Hours, but its last for a long time. It was the North American Racing Team that saved the honour of the Maranello firm, whose works prototypes were eliminated one after the other. This year marked the triumph of the private teams: NART's win was matched by the Francorchamps team's victory in the GT class.

Ferrari no. 21. Type 250 LM, Prototype (chassis no. 5893 GT), entered by North American Racing Team, driven by Gregory and Rindt. It was first on distance, covering 4677.110km (2906.221 miles) at an average 194.880km/h (121.093mph).
With the stars eliminated the crowd witnessed a duel between 250 LMs: the red of NART against the yellow of the Ecurie Francorchamps. It was the former that took the event, after a thrilling finish. After being held back at the start the old American and the young Austrian pushed on hard and fast to the finish, giving Luigi Chinetti a superb victory and cocking a tremendous snook at the works Fords and Ferraris.

Ferrari no. 26. Type 250 LM, Prototype (chassis no. 6313 GT), entered by Ecurie Francorchamps, driven by Dumay and Gosselin. It came second on distance, covering 4602.600km (2859.923 miles) at an average 191.775km/h (119.163mph).

Pierre Dumay and Taf Gosselin, both purely amateur, battled right to the finish in their private 250 LM against two skilled professional drivers in an identical car: and they came close to beating them. At 1.00pm the yellow car burst a tyre at the Hunaudières, destroying the right-hand rear wing. Gosselin returned at reduced speed to the pits but the race was decided. It cost time to do the repairs; Gregory and Rindt were way ahead and the Belgian car had to be content with holding on to its second place at the end.

Ferrari no. 24. Type 275 GTB, category GT (chassis no. 6885 GT), entered by Ecurie Francorchamps, driven by W. Mairesse and 'Beurlys'. It was third on distance, covering 4562.050km (2834.726 miles) at an average 190.085km/h (118.113mph).

This car carried all Ferrari's hopes in the GT class, in contention with five Cobras. It was above all thanks to the skill of Willy Mairesse that this imperfect car was able to put up such a performance. Problems with excessive and unexpected overheating affected this rather ugly car during the race.

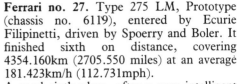

Ferrari no. 27. Type 275 LM, Prototype (chassis no. 6119), entered by Ecurie Filipinetti, driven by Spoerry and Boler. It finished sixth on distance, covering 4354.160km (2705.550 miles) at an average 181.423km/h (112.731mph).

A good sixth place, after a very intelligent effort, illustrates the proverb 'More haste, less speed'.

Ferrari no. 18. Type 365 P2, Prototype (chassis no. 0838), entered by North American Racing Team, driven by P. Rodriguez and Vaccarella. It was seventh on distance, covering 4300.190km (2672.014 miles) at an average 179.175km/h (111.334mph).

Rodriguez was soon complaining of lack of power in his car and experienced all the difficulties of the P2s – brakes and then the transmission – which explains his less than brilliant performance. Nevertheless the car won the 4–5 litres class.

Ferrari no. 20. Type 330 P2, Prototype (chassis no. 0836), entered by SEFAC-Ferrari, driven by Guichet and Parkes. It retired in the 23rd hour, after being fifth in the 22nd hour.

Three hours into the event, and with the Fords held up, it was this Franco-British team that took the lead ahead of three other Ferraris. Unfortunately this 330 P2 had to spend a whole 50 minutes in the pits while two broken brake discs were replaced. As on car number 19, the gearbox suffered from its intensive use and the two drivers proceeded round slowly with it jammed in fifth before retiring.

Ferrari no. 19. Type 330 P2, Prototype (chassis no. 0828), entered by SEFAC-Ferrari, driven by Surtees and Scarfiotti. It retired in the 18th hour, after being in 10th place in the preceding hour.

This was the fastest of the Ferrari teams, but the pair were held back by brake problems, as with all the P2s. To make them last out they used the gearbox for slowing down, but it could not stand up to such rough treatment.

Ferrari no. 22. Type 275 P2, Prototype (chassis no. 0832), entered by SEFAC-Ferrari, driven by Bandini and Biscaldi. It retired in the ·17th hour with a broken valve after being in 11th place in the preceding hour.

Ferrari no. 25. Type 250 LM, Prototype (chassis no. 6023), entered by Ecurie Francorchamps, driven by Langlois and 'Eldé'. It retired in the 12th hour with clutch trouble after being in 15th place.

Ferrari no. 17. Type 365 P2, Prototype (chassis no. 0826), entered by Maranello Concessionaires Ltd, driven by Bonnier and Piper. It retired in the ninth hour, after being in 23rd place in the preceding hour. Well placed among the leading bunch of Ferraris, this 365 P2 was held back by a defective exhaust manifold. Exhaust gases continuously seeping into the cockpit forced this team to give up during the night.

Ferrari no. 23. Type 275 LM, Prototype (chassis no. 5895), entered by Maranello Concessionaires Ltd, driven by L. Bianchi and Salmon. It retired in the eighth hour, after being in 12th position in the preceding hour: its gearbox shattered at 10.30pm.

Ferrari no. 40. Type Dino 166, Prototype (chassis no. 0834), entered by SEFAC-Ferrari, driven by Baghetti and Casoni. It retired in the first hour.
Baghetti missed a gear change on his fifth lap. As a result a valve was bent and Casoni lost his chance of driving the Dino.

1966

Fourteen Ferraris start, two finish

Victory for Ford who, in the presence of Henry Ford II, put three Mark IIs in three first places. A disaster for Ferrari with only two cars managing to finish – fortunately one of them took the GT class. In the end the great winner was the Automobile Club de l'Ouest which, because of the titanic Ford–Ferrari duel, attracted more spectators than ever to its circuit.

The winners of the event were MacLaren and Amon in a Ford MkII, at an average speed of 201.795km/h (125.390mph) over a distance of 4843.090km (3009.357 miles).

Ferrari no. 29. Type 275 GTB, category GT (chassis no. 09035 GT), entered by Maranello Concessionaires Ltd, driven by Courage and Pike. It came eighth in the distance placings, covering 4212.500km (2617.526 miles) at an average 175.521km/h (109.064mph).
This was the first (and last-but-one) Ferrari to be placed this year. Roy Pike and Piers Courage, two Formula 3 hopes, thus saved the Ferrari honour.

Ferrari no. 57. Type 275 GTB, category GT (chassis no. 09027 GT), entered by Ecurie Francorchamps, driven by Noblet and Dubois. It was 10th on distance, covering 4171.620km (2592.125 miles) at an average 173.818km/h (108.005mph).
Experience paid off for these two northern Frenchmen who finished, but a long way behind the winners.

Ferrari no. 26. Type 275 GTB, category GT (chassis no. 9015), entered by North American Racing Team, driven by Biscaldi and de Bourbon Parma. It retired in the 20th hour with clutch trouble after being in seventh place in the preceding hour.

Ferrari no. 21. Type 330 P3, Prototype (chassis no. 0844), entered by North American Racing Team, driven by Bandini and Guichet. It retired in the 17th hour, after being in 11th place in the preceding hour. These two former Le Mans 24 Hours winners were no luckier than their team mates, damaging their gearbox, having brake trouble then finally pulling out because of a blown cylinder head gasket.

Ferrari no. 28. Type 250 LM, Sports (chassis no. 6023), entered by the Belgian national team, driven by Gosselin and de Keyn. It retired with gasket trouble in the 18th hour, after being in 13th position in the preceding hour.

Ferrari no. 17. Type 365 P2, Prototype (chassis no. 0828), entered by Ecurie Francorchamps, driven by 'Beurlys' and Dumay. It gave up in the 14th hour with gasket trouble, after being in 14th place in the preceding hour.

Ferrari no. 19. Type 365 P2, Prototype (chassis no. 0832), entered by Scuderia Filipinetti, driven by W. Mairesse and Müller. It withdrew in the 12th hour, after lying in 15th place in the preceding hour.
In a flood of retirements this Swiss P2 had the privilege for a while of being the leading Ferrari. In the end the gearbox decided things otherwise.

Ferrari no. 27. Type 330 P3, Prototype, entered by North American Racing Team, driven by P. Rodriguez and Ginther. It retired in the 11th hour, after occupying fourth place in the preceding hour.

This crack team achieved the best time of all the Ferraris with 3′ 33sec, although this was well behind that of Gurney's Ford (3′ 30.6sec). In the event it was again the best of them, spinning along behind the Fords and briefly going to the front before the gearbox gave up and forced the Americans to pull out at 1.45am.

Ferrari no. 18. Type 365 P2, Prototype (chassis no. 0838), entered by North American Racing Team, driven by Gregory and Bondurant. It retired in the ninth hour, after lying in 36th position in the preceding hour. This car had been partly destroyed by fire at Sebring and reconditioned for Le Mans, and fitted with a 'long-tailed' rear end made in Italy by Drogo. A broken transmission compelled this somewhat elderly white Ferrari to withdraw.

Ferrari no. 20. Type 330 P3, Prototype, entered by SEFAC-Ferrari, driven by Scarfiotti and Parkes. It retired in the ninth hour, after being in fifth place in the preceding hour.

Scarfiotti, avoiding a CD across the track at the Tertre-Rouge, went off the road and collided violently with the barriers, which forced him to withdraw.

Ferrari no. 38. Type Dino 206, Prototype (chassis no. 008), entered by North American Racing Team, driven by Kolb and Follmer. It retired in the third hour, after occupying 15th place in the preceding hour.

The three Dinos had been given the nod to withdraw from the opening stages of the event. The engine gave out on this car, which had been running at the bottom of its category.

Ferrari no. 36. Type Dino 206, Prototype, entered by Maranello Concessionaires Ltd, driven by Salmon and Hobbs. It withdrew in the third hour, after lying in 49th place in the preceding hour.

It was the transmission that failed on this British Dino.

Ferrari no. 16. Type 365 P2, Prototype (chassis no. 0826), entered by Maranello Concessionaires Ltd, driven by Attwood and Piper. It retired in the third hour after occupying 46th position in the previous hour.

This was the first P2 to withdraw (after the three Dinos) in this year's Le Mans 24 Hours, in which Ferrari did not exactly shine. The two drivers gave up finally after courageously making 28 laps of the circuit – at reduced speed.

Ferrari no. 25. Type Dino 206, Prototype (chassis no. 014), entered by North American Racing Team, driven by Casoni and Vaccerella. It retired in the third hour, after being in 55th place in the preceding hour. The engine gave out – as with the other NART Dino, and practically at the same time.

1967

Nine Ferraris start, three finish

With its P4, Ferrari was responding to the superiority of the victorious Fords at the previous year's Le Mans 24 Hours. The Americans put three Mk IIs into three first places, but the Porsches could be seen coming up over the horizon, asserting themselves year by year, and also a newcomer who was being talked about: Matra.

The winners of the event were Gurney and Foyt in their Ford Mk IV at an average speed of 218.038km/h (135.483mph) over 5232.900km (3251.573 miles).

Ferrari no. 21. Type P4, Prototype (chassis no. 0858), entered by SEFAC-Ferrari, driven by Scarfiotti and Parkes. It was placed second on distance, covering 5180.590km (3219.069 miles) at an average 215.858km/h (134.128mph).
The battle to gain this second place was a rough one. Skill (and a heavy foot on the pedal) paid off once more and all the records were broken. The fuel consumption of this P4 went up to 40,864 litres/100km during the event. Its range on 140 litres was 25 laps or 340km.

Ferrari no. 24. Type P4, Prototype (chassis no. 0856), entered by the Belgian national team, driven by Mairesse and 'Beurlys'. It came in third on distance, covering 5084.390km (3159.294 miles) at an average 211.850km/h (131.637mph).
Another splendid performance from Willy Mairesse, who finished some 100km (62 miles) behind the works P4, which was 2nd.

Ferrari no. 28. Type 275 GTB, category GT, entered by Scuderia Filipinetti, driven by Steinnemann and Spoerry. It finished 11th on distance, covering 4281.000km (2660.090 miles) at an average 178.375km/h (110.837mph).
It won the GT category after an unrelenting battle with its Corvette and Porsche peers, achieving an average time that would have brought it the overall first place seven years before.

Ferrari no. 19. Type P4, Prototype (chassis no. 0860), entered by SEFAC-Ferrari, driven by Klass and Sutcliffe. It retired in the 18th hour, after lying in 17th place in the preceding hour.
This car, which was in an accident in practice, drove a very consistent race until its withdrawal at 11am on the Sunday with a damaged injection pump.

Ferrari no. 23. Type 412 P, Prototype (chassis no. 0854), entered by Maranello Concessionaires Ltd, driven by Attwood and Courage. It retired in the 15th hour, after being in ninth place in the preceding hour.
The Britons were battling for eighth place 15 laps behind the leaders when a piston went through the crankcase.

Ferrari no. 20. Type P4, Prototype (chassis no. 0846), entered by SEFAC-Ferrari, driven by Amon and Vaccarella. It withdrew in the eighth hour after being in 13th position in the preceding hour.
This was the only open-bodied car out of the 54 lined up at the start. Early in the night, when it had been lying second for a lap, Chris Amon burst a tyre at the entry to the Hunaudières bend. A fire started in his car while he was trying to regain the pits. The flames were soon contained, but unfortunately retirement was now unavoidable.

Ferrari no. 25. Type 412 P, Prototype (chassis no. 0844), entered by North American Racing Team, driven by P. Rodriguez and Baghetti. It retired in the 11th hour, after being in 16th place in the preceding hour.
For several hours this Ferrari showed disturbing signs of inadequacy. It finally pulled out during the night with a cracked piston.

Ferrari no. 22. Type 412 P3/4, Prototype (chassis no. 0848), entered by Scuderia Filipinetti, driven by Guichet and Müller. It gave up in the seventh hour, after being in 21st position in the preceding hour. An oil leak obliged this 412 P to withdraw.

Ferrari no. 26. Type 365 P2, Prototype (chassis no. 0838), entered by North American Racing Team, driven by Pearson and R. Rodriguez. It retired in the fourth hour, after occupying 45th place in the preceding hour.

The American Rodriguez (no relation of Pedro) went into the sand at Mulsanne after taking over from his compatriot Chuck Pearson. After struggling for an hour he had to give up and withdraw. Note that number 0838 was taking part in its third successive Le Mans 24 Hours.

1968

Six Ferraris start, one finishes

The events that shook France in the month of May 1968 compelled the ACO to postpone the Le Mans 24 Hours until September. Again it was Ford who carried it off, for the third year running. Of the Ferraris, only a single car reached the finish. It was a long way from the great duels of old.

The winners of the event, Pedro Rodriguez and Lucien Bianchi, drove their Ford GT 40 at an average of 185.536km/h (115.287mph) for a distance of 4452.880km (2766.891 miles).

Ferrari no. 21. Type 250 LM, Sports (chassis no. 8165), entered by David Piper, driven by Piper and Attwood. It was seventh on distance, covering 4060.390km (2523.009 miles) at an average 169.182km/h (105.125mph).
This old green Ferrari was kept back by engine overheating and by whimsical ignition. Be that as it may, the Englishmen drove an intelligent race, slowed up by a number of troubles: an oil leak, a water leak, and a short circuit. This LM was the last to leave the factory.

Ferrari no. 19. Type 275 LM, Sports (chassis no. 6167), entered by Paul Vestey, driven by Vestey and Pike. It retired in the 11th hour, after being in 31st position in the preceding hour.
A slight shunt, then electrical problems, slowed this not-very-fast 275 LM. In the end the gearbox gave up, forcing the drivers to do the same.

Ferrari no. 20. Type 250 LM, Sports (chassis no. 5891), entered by Scuderia Filipinetti, driven by Müller and Williams. It retired in the 18th hour, after being in ninth place in the preceding hour, with a wheel jammed and the cardan joint gone.

Ferrari no. 14. Type 250 LM, Sports (chassis no. 5893), entered by North American Racing Team, driven by Gregory and Kolb. It retired in the 18th hour, after lying in 10th place in the preceding hour.

Masten Gregory was this year driving the car in which he and Rindt had won the 1965 event. Gregory's talent raised illusory hopes for a while but the car was too old and poorly prepared. Its clutch caused the team a lot of worry. Finally Charlie Kolb negated all Gregory's efforts by going off the road at Tertre-Rouge and returning on foot to disqualification.

Ferrari no. 17. Type 275 GTB, category GT (chassis no.09079), entered by Scuderia Filipinetti, driven by Rey and Haldi. It withdrew in the eighth hour, after occupying 35th position the previous hour.
The car was in 44th place on the first lap and then was neatly overtaken by the Porsche it was competing with in its class. In the end Rey drove the GTB into the barriers on the Indianapolis curve.

Ferrari no. 36. Type Dino 206 S, category GT, entered by North American Racing Team, driven by Chevalier and Lagier. It gave up in the seventh hour, after being in 42nd place in the preceding hour.
This was the third year that Luigi Chinetti entered a car for Le Mans for the sake of young French hopefuls. The car for 1968 does not seem to have been prepared well enough for the event, which in this team's case was early interrupted by a blown gasket.

1969

Four Ferraris start, one finishes

A very feeble participation by Ferrari in the Le Mans 24 Hours this year, when the marque went unnoticed. Reading the list of winners made it clear that Ford, marking up its fourth consecutive victory, was passing the torch to Porsche and that Matra was coming to the front.

The winners of the event were Ickx and Oliver in a Ford GT 40, with 4998.000km (3105.613 miles) at an average speed of 208.250km/h (129.401mph).

Ferrari no. 17. Type 250 LM, Sports (chassis no. 5893; registration no. XD 612), entered by North American Racing Team, driven by Zeccoli and Posey. It finished eighth on distance, covering 4424.050km (2748.977 miles) at an average 184.335km/h (114.540mph).
In the elderly 5893, winner in 1965, Sam Posey and Teodoro Zeccoli lasted out the course and achieved an honourable placing, considering the age and the condition of their car.

Ferrari no. 18. Type 312 P, Sports Prototype (chassis no. 0870), entered by SEFAC-Ferrari, driven by P. Rodriguez and Piper. It retired in the 16th hour, after being in eighth place in the preceding hour.
The two drivers were held back by gearbox troubles and an oil leak. Despite its 420 bhp, the 312 P was never fast enough to hope to do well.

Ferrari no. 59. Type 275 GTB, category GT (chassis no. 09079; registration no. GE 51180), entered by Scuderia Filipinetti, driven by Rey and Haldi. It was disqualified in the fifth hour, after occupying 35th place in the preceding hour.
In its third participation in the Le Mans 24 Hours this GTB did not have the chance of finishing: it was stopped by the steward for topping up its oil too early.

Ferrari no. 19. Type 312 P, Sports Prototype (chassis no. 0868), entered by SEFAC-Ferrari, driven by Amon and Schetty.

This Ferrari, with Chris Amon at the wheel, did not complete its first lap. At Maison-Blanche Woolfe's Porsche 917 hit the barriers and caught fire. Amon, who was following the 917, ran into its fuel tank which had been torn from the Porsche's chassis in the impact. Chris Amon succeeded in getting out of his burning car and returned on foot to the pits. John Woolfe, the driver of the 917, died in the accident.

Ferrari no. 61. Type Dino, category GT (chassis no. 014), entered by North American Racing Team. Jimmy Mieusset was to share the steering wheel with another young French hopeful François Migault, within the provisions of the Trophée Chinetti.

This car passed the weight tests but did not take part in the event. When it was being driven in practice by Grossman it collided at Mulsanne with the Ferrari Daytona from the same team, with Ricardo Rodriguez at the wheel. Neither of these NART cars was able to compete.

Ferrari no. 16. Type Daytona, Sports (chassis no. 12547), entered by North American Racing Team; R. Rodriguez was to drive.

This aluminium Daytona went from Maranello to Le Mans by road, crossing the Alps by night with Luigi Chinetti himself at the wheel. Unfortunately the two American drivers collided with each other at Mulsanne and neither the Daytona nor the Dino was able to run in the event.

1970

Twelve Ferraris start, three finish

The first victory for a Porsche in the Le Mans 24 Hours. Ferrari may have made itself felt in the first year of its participation, but it took Porsche 19 years to do the same. Faced with the formidable German 917s, the Ferrari 512s were shown to be less effective. It should be noted that these two marques shared the seven placed cars between them.

The winners of the event were Attwood and Herrmann in a Porsche 917: 4607.810km (2863.160 miles) at an average 191.992km/h (119.298mph).

Ferrari no. 11. Type 512 S, Sports (chassis no. 1014), entered by North American Racing Team, driven by Posey and Buckman. It finished fourth on distance, covering 4209.600km (2615.724 miles) at an average 175.400km/h (108.989mph).

This was the first Ferrari placed, behind three Porsches. It should be remembered that the 512s were created in less than nine months to try and counteract the striking superiority of the Porsche 917s. For the 1970 Le Mans Ferrari lined up no fewer than twelve 512s, official and non-official. This American team struggled all through the event with roadholding that was never up to the mark.

Ferrari no. 12. Type 512 S, Sports (chassis no. 1030), entered by Ecurie Francorchamps, driven by Walker and de Fierlant. It came fifth on distance, covering 4103.520km (2549.809 miles) at an average 170.980km/h (106.242mph).

A good performance from this Belgian Ferrari which got back into the general placings thanks to the skill of its drivers (and numerous retirements). It is worth noting that few Le Mans 24 Hours have seen such a spate of withdrawals. In 1931 only six teams were placed; this year there were seven!

Ferrari no. 57. Type 312 P, Sports Prototype (chassis no. 0872), entered by North American Racing Team, driven by Parsons and Adamovicz. It was not placed.

The car was in sixth place when serious ignition troubles pulled it back. It did finally struggle over the finishing line but it was not placed as it had not covered a sufficient distance. Its technical problems, and also the awful weather, were responsible.

Ferrari no. 16. Type 512 S, Sports (chassis no. 1032), entered by Scuderia Filipinetti, driven by Manfredini and Moretti. It retired with a damaged transmission in the third hour, after being in 28th place in the preceding hour.

Ferrari no. 9. Type 512 S, Sports (chassis no. 1002), entered by Escuderia Montjuich, driven by Juncadella and Fernandez. It went out in the 11th hour, after occupying 10th place in the preceding hour.
The Spaniard Juncadella damaged the front of his Ferrari in an accident.

Ferrari no. 10. Type 512, S, Sports (chassis no. 1018), entered by North American Racing Team, driven by Kelleners and Loos. It retired in the seventh hour as the result of an accident, after being logged in 38th place in the preceding hour.

Ferrari no. 5. Type 512 S, Sports (chassis no. 1038), entered by SEFAC-Ferrari, driven by Ickx and Schetty. It went out in the 11th hour, after lying in fifth place in the preceding hour.

Jacky Ickx, who had been answering the challenge of the very fast Porsche 917s, lost his brakes during the 10th hour on the approach to Maison-Blanche. It was probably a wheel locking that threw the Ferrari off balance and it ran into a heap of sand that was too damp to stop it. The 512 S shot off what in effect became a springboard, killing a track steward.

Ferrari no. 7. Type 512 S, Sports (chassis no. 1026), entered by SEFAC-Ferrari, driven by Bell and Peterson. It retired in the fourth hour, after being logged in 24th place in the preceding hour.

Ferrari number 7 was one of four 512Ss involved in the accident on the Maison-Blanche approach. Derek Bell did not hit anyone, but put paid to his engine while trying to extricate himself.

Ferrari no. 8. Type 512 S, Sports (chassis no. 1034), entered by SEFAC-Ferrari, driven by Merzario and Regazzoni. It went out in the fourth hour, after being in 26th place in the preceding hour.

One bad manoeuvre and a surface made very slippery by the rain caused the retirement of four Ferrari 512s. It seems to have been the fiery Clay who was responsible for this pile-up, which did the Porsche cause a lot of good.

Ferrari no. 14. Type 512 S, Sports (chassis no. 1008), entered by Scuderia Filipinetti, driven by Bonnier and Wissel. It retired in the fourth hour, after occupying 35th place in the preceding hour.

Reine Wissel, who was travelling at low speed, was struck by the Clay-Regazzoni 512 S and had to abandon the event.

Ferrari no. 15. Type 512 S, sports (chassis no. 1016), entered by Scuderia Filipinetti, driven by Parkes and Müller. It went out in the fourth hour, after being in 29th position in the preceding hour.

Michael Parkes was unable to avoid the two Ferraris blocking the track at Maison-Blanche. He was slightly burned in a fire that was quickly brought under control.

Ferrari no. 6. Type 512 S, Sports (chassis no. 1044), entered by SEFAC-Ferrari, driven by Giunti and Vaccarella.
This car achieved the second-fastest time in practice (3′20sec), two-tenths away from that set by Elford in a 917. In the seventh lap Vaccarella returned to the pits at a low speed with a broken conrod.

1971

Ten Ferraris start, three finish

Porsche's 2nd victory in the Le Mans 24 Hours, which once again witnessed the crushing superiority of the German firm. In the absence of works entries, the Ferrari response to the Porsche 917 was inconclusive, depsite the third and fourth places in the general classification. It was a pity for Ferrari that the first Daytona was not homologated for the GT category, where it would otherwise have given itself a victory.

The winners of the event were Marko and Van Lennep in a Porsche 917 with 5335.313km (3315.210 miles) at an average 222.304km/h (138.133mph).

Ferrari no. 12. Type 512 M, Sports (chassis no. 1020), entered by North American Racing Team, driven by Posey and Adamovicz. It came third on distance, covering 4922.090km (3058.445 miles) at an average 205.087km/h (127.435mph).

This was the first Ferrari placed (400km – 250 miles – behind the winners nonetheless). There was one alarm in the last laps to disturb Sam and Tony: a broken shock absorber.

Ferrari no. 16. Type 512 M, Sports (chassis no. 1028), entered by David Piper, driven by Craft and Wier. It finished fourth on distance, covering 4768.138km (2962.784 miles) at an average 198.672km/h (123.449mph).

That this 512 figured in the placings was a miracle: various carburation problems slowed it down, then the clutch had to be changed. In the final laps of the course the clutch again showed signs of fatigue.

Ferrari no. 58. Type 365 GTB 4, Sports (chassis no. 12467), entered by North American Racing Team, driven by Grossman and Chinetti Jr. It came fifth on distance, covering 4218.752km (2621.411 miles) at an average 175.781km/h (109.225mph).

'Coco' Chinetti, son of the three-times winner of Le Mans, had the privilege of being the first to drive the Daytona on this circuit. After a consistent race, Bob and 'Coco' won their class in the Index of Thermal Efficiency ahead of the Porsche outright winners. It should be noted that the Daytona was entered in the Sports category while awaiting homologation for GT (in face it finished in front of the victorious Porsche in GT).

Ferrari no. 9. Type 512 M, Sports (chassis no. 1030), entered by Ecurie Francorchamps, driven by de Fierlant and de Cadenet. It retired in the 18th hour, after lying in seventh place in the preceding hour. First delayed by having to change the clutch, this Anglo-Belgian team finally had to give up because of the same problem.

Ferrari no. 6. Type 512 M, Sports (chassis no. 1032), entered by Scuderia Filipinetti, driven by Manfredini and Gagliardi. It retired in the 17th hour, with a damaged gearbox, after being in 11th place in the preceding hour.

Ferrari no. 15. Type 512 M, Sports (chassis no. 1002), entered by Escuderia Montjuich, driven by Vaccarella and Juncadella. It retired in the 14th hour, after being in fifth place the previous hour.
Nino Vaccarella and his partner José Maria Juncadella put in a superb performance, up at the front and a lap ahead just before they sustained damage to their transmission.

Ferrari no. 7. Type 512 F, Sports (chassis no. 1048), entered by Scuderia Filipinetti, driven by Parkes and Pescarolo. It went out in the 13th hour, after lying in 29th position in the preceding hour.
Michael Parkes modified this car for the Filipinetti team, and this explains the 'F' after the type number. Parkes left the road at Maison-Blanche, damaging the body panels fore and aft. In the end loss of oil pressure forced their retirement.

Ferrari no. 10. Type 512 M, Sports (chassis no. 1018), entered by Gelo Racing Team, driven by Loos and Pesch. It retired in the sixth hour with a broken conrod, after occupying 16th place in the preceding hour.

Ferrari no. 11. Type 512 M, Sports (chassis no. 1040), entered by North American Racing Team, driven by Donohue and Hobbs. It retired in the sixth hour, after being in 14th place in the preceding hour.
The 'Sunoco' was involved in the struggle at the front in the early hours. Unfortunately it made a long pit stop at the start of the fifth hour. Once the beginning of a seizure was diagnosed the handsome blue and yellow Ferrari was pushed behind the pits. This 512 had been the fastest of the Ferraris in practice.

Ferrari no. 14. Type 512 S, Sports (chassis no. 1006), entered by North American Racing Team, driven by Gregory and Eaton. It withdrew in the fifth hour, after occupying 46th position in the preceding hour.
Continuing carburation troubles got the better of this elderly American 512.

1972

Ten Ferraris start, six finish

The first victory in the Le Mans 24 Hours for Matra, who took over from Porsche at the top of the podium. In the GT category, by way of revenge, Ferrari crushed its opponents – the German firm among them – putting five Daytonas in the first five places.

The winners of the event·were Pescarolo and Graham Hill in their Matra 670 with 4691.343km (2915.065 miles) at an average speed of 195.472km/h (121.461mph).

Ferrari no. 39. Type 365 GTB 4, category GTS, entered by Pozzi-France, driven by Andruet, Ballot and Léna. It came fifth on distance, covering 4162.660km (2586.557 miles) at an average 173.444km/h (107.773mph).
Chronometers in the heads of the drivers, and an impeccable race schedule, brought victory in the GT class to this Ferrari, entered (for the first time) by the French importer Charles Pozzi. In addition his team got themselves into first place in the Index of Thermal Efficiency. This was the fastest Daytona on the Hunaudières straight, where it was timed at 296km/h (183.926mph).

Ferrari no. 74. Type 365 GTB 4, category GTS, entered by North American Racing Team, driven by Posey and Adamovicz. It was sixth on distance covering 4137.733km (2571.068 miles) at an average 172.405km/h (107.128mph).
The fight to win the GT category put this American team into competition with the Ferrari-France partnership of Andruet, Ballot and Léna. Sam Posey went too fast into the Indianapolis turn and ended up facing the wrong way. His gearbox was damaged in the process – and the Frenchmen were to have no further worries.

Ferrari no. 34. Type 365 GTB 4, category GTS, entered by Scuderia Filipinetti, driven by Parkes, Lafosse and Cochet. It came seventh on distance, covering 4110.051km (2553.867 miles) at an average 171.252km/h (106.411mph).
A fine third place in the GT category came to this somewhat mixed team.

Ferrari no. 46. Type Dino 246 GT, category GTS, entered by North American Racing Team, driven by Laffeach and Doncieux. It was placed 17th on distance, covering 3602.988km (2238.793 miles) at an average 150.124km/h (93.283mph).
This traditional Trophée Chinetti Dino was first substitute when a withdrawal sanctioned its participation.

Ferrari no. 36. Type 365 GTB 4, category GTS, entered by Ecurie Francorchamps, driven by Bell, T. Pilette and Bond. It achieved eighth place on distance, covering 4109.864km (2553.751 miles) at an average 171.244km/h (106.406mph).
The progress of this star team (Bell and Pilette) was held back a little by Richard Bond, who drove two stages in the night.

Ferrari no. 38. Type 365 GTB 4, category GTS, entered by North American Racing team, driven by Jarier and C. Buchet. It was ninth on distance, covering 4039.443km (2509.994 miles) at an average 168.310km/h (104.583mph).

Ferrari no. 57. Type 365 GTB 4, category GTS, entered by North American Racing Team, driven by Gregory and Chinetti Jr. It retired in the 20th hour, after being in 19th place in the preceding hour, due to gearbox damage early in the night.

Ferrari no. 35. Type 365 GTB 4, category GTS, entered by Scuderia Filipinetti, driven by Chenevière, Vetsch and Pillon. It went out in the 18th hour, after lying in 25th place in the preceding hour.
Florian Vetsch was in collision with Jo Bonnier in the small hours in the Indianapolis bend and had to retire.

Ferrari no. 37. Type 365 GTB 4, category GTS, entered by Maranello Concessionnaires Ltd, driven by Westbury and Hine. It retired with a cracked piston in the ninth hour, after being in 29th place in the preceding hour.
This car, entered by the British Ferrari importer, was fitted with right-hand drive.

Ferrari no. 75. Type 365 GTB 4, category GTS, entered by Pozzi-France, driven by Migault and Rouveyran. It withdrew in the eighth hour, after occupying 44th position in the preceding hour.
This was the fastest Ferrari in practice, with 4'21.7sec, but it was bettered by another GT, the Corvette driven by Darniche. After being in the lead in its category, its gearbox jammed and repairs took an hour and a half.

1973

Twelve Ferraris start, five finish

This year was the 50th anniversary of the Le Mans 24 Hours, which had started in 1923. The ACO wanted to mark the occasion with an enticing poster: the Matra–Ferrari duel.

This duel went in favour of the French, although the Ferrari 312s had seemed faster in practice. A consolation for Ferrari was its GT victory over the Porsche RSRs. The winning team was Henri Pescarolo and Gerard Larrousse in their Matra 670 B, at an average 202.247km/h (125.670mph) for a distance of 4853.945km (3016.102 miles).

Ferrari no. 16. Type 312 P/B, Sports, entered by SEFAC Ferrari, driven by Merzario and Pace. It came second on distance, covering 4772.290km (2965.364 miles) at an average 198.845km/h (123.557mph). It achieved the best time in practice with 3′ 37.5sec, better by one second than the Ickx-Redman Ferrari.

The car made a flying start, staying at the front for the first two hours. Then a problem with the fuel feed slowed down Carlos Pace, who found himself soaked in petrol in his cockpit. It took half an hour to dry out. Then at 1.15am Pace stopped to change the clutch, which was slipping, which cost 40 minutes. Finally this team benefited from the withdrawal of Ickx and Redman, and secured its second place.

Ferrari no. 39. Type 365 GTB 4, category GTS (chassis no. 16363), entered by Pozzi-France, driven by Elford, Ballot and Léna. It was sixth on distance, covering 4321.341km (2685.157 miles) at an average 180.055km/h (111.882mph).
A recalcitrant brake component cost this team 11 minutes but it nevertheless won the GT class. The car developed 440 bhp and was the fastest Daytona in practice with 4' 16.2sec.

Ferrari no. 40. Type 365 GTB 4,category GTS (chassis no. 15667), entered by Pozzi-France, driven by Serpaggi and Dolhem. It finished ninth on distance, covering 4309.461km (2677.775 miles) at an average 179.561km/h (111.573mph).
José Dolhem was suffering from lumbago for a good part of the race. The team completed the event without incident and came second in the Index of Thermal Efficiency.

Ferrari no. 38. Type 365 GTB 4, category GTS (chassis no. 13141), entered by North American Racing Team, driven by Migault and Chinetti Jr. It was placed 13th on distance, covering 4078.527km (2534.279 miles) at an average 169.939km/h (105.595mph).
An event without problems for the Frenchman and for the son of Luigi, three times winner of Le Mans.

Ferrari no. 34. Type 365 GTB 4, category GTS (chassis no. 16425), entered by Ecurie Francorchamps, driven by Andruet and Bond. It came 20th on distance, covering 3693.048km (2294.754 miles) at an average 153.877km/h (95.147mph).
There were a lot of minor troubles for this Belgian team, which finished 46 laps behind the winners in its class.

Ferrari no. 15. Type 312 P/B, Sports, entered by SEFAC-Ferrari, driven by Ickx and Redman. It retired in the final hour, after being in third place in the preceding hour.
The contest between this Ferrari and the Larrousse-Pescarolo Matra was a thrilling one. A broken silencer meant a loss of power and time for the Ferrari. It was on the same lap as the Matra when it suffered the mishap that had occurred to Merzario earlier – a fuel leak. Jacky Ickx had to change his overalls, letting the Matra get four laps ahead. Finally, at 2.27am, Ickx slowly returned to the pits with a conrod gone.

Ferrari no. 6. Type 365 GTB 4, category GTS (chassis no. 16407), entered by North American Racing Team, driven by Posey and Minter. It withdrew in the 21st hour, after being in 14th position in the preceding hour.
This team dominated the GTS competition until the moment that the engine gave out with a cracked piston.

Ferrari no. 36. Type 365 GTB 4, category GTS (chassis no. 14889), entered by North American Racing Team, driven by Grossman and Guitteny. It retired in the 19th hour, after lying in 26th place in the preceding hour.
There was no chance for this Daytona which had to pull into the pits at the end of the warm-up lap with a split tyre. Later, a little after midnight, Bob Grossman went off the road, damaged the car and had to withdraw.

Ferrari no. 33. Type 365 GTB 4, category GTS (chassis no. 15681), entered by J. C. Bamford Excavator Ltd, driven by Corner and Green. It went out in the 18th hour, after being in 17th position in the preceding hour.
Green crashed into the barriers, damaging this Italian beauty, then the clutch packed up completely.

Ferrari no. 37. Type 365 GTB 4, category GTS (chassis no. 16367), entered by North American Racing Team, driven by Di Palma and Garcia Veiga. It withdrew in the 18th hour, after being in 20th place in the preceding hour.

It was clutch trouble that stopped these Argentinians who, until this happened, had driven very consistently.

Ferrari no. 56. Type 365 GTB 4, category GTS (chassis no. 14407), entered by Shark Team, driven by Gueurie and Grandet. It withdrew in the 17th hour, after being in 29th position during the preceding hour: the gearbox was the cause.

Earlier on, leaving the road and trouble with the fuel pump had already delayed this car considerably.

Ferrari no. 17. Type 312 P/B, Sports, entered by SEFAC-Ferrari, driven by Reutemann and Schenken. It retired in the 12th hour, after lying in third place in the preceding hour.

The slowest of the 312s in practice, it ran a very shrewd race which took it to the top of the general classification for several hours. Unfortunately Reutemann had to return to the pits in a cloud of smoke with his engine gone.

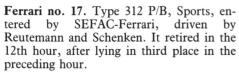

1974

Seven Ferraris start, five finish

The third, and last, Matra victory in the Le Mans 24 Hours; and the third victory for the great Henri Pescarolo who was in the right car each time. He had to wait ten years before mounting the podium there again. The Daytonas were starting to show their years, their fine achievements notwithstanding. The GT victory went to one of them, which finished fifth on distance.

The winners were Pescarolo and Larrousse in their Matra 670B, with an average speed of 191.940km/h (119.266mph) over 4646.571km (2862.391 miles).

Ferrari no. 71. Type 365 GTB, category GTS (chassis no. 14407), entered by R. Touroul, driven by Grandet and Bardini. It came fifth on distance, covering 4280.505km (2659.783 miles) at an average 178.354km/h (110.824mph).

People thought that the Porsches were going to make short work of the ageing Daytonas – forgetting that there are no 'certs' or foregone conclusions at Le Mans and that the V12 Ferrari was sound and strong.

First place in the GTS category, first in the Index of Thermal Efficiency, first in the 3–5 litres class – this was enough for this French team which completed 313 laps.

Ferrari no. 54. Type 365 GTB 4, category GTS (chassis no. 14141), entered by North American Racing Team, driven by Heinz and Cudini. It was sixth on distance, covering 4262.238km (2648.432 miles) at an average 177.593km/h (110.351mph).

Second in the Index of Thermal Efficiency, second in GTS, second in the 3–5 litres class – this Daytona finished in the shadow of the number 71 Ferrari.

Ferrari no. 1. Type 312 P, Sports, entered by North American Racing Team, driven by Zeccoli and Andruet. It finished ninth on distance, covering 4071.650km (2530.006 miles) at an average 169.652km/h (105.417mph).

This old 312 fitted with a V engine (and not a 'Boxer') broke six accelerator cables but was creditably placed in 5th in the 13th and 14th hours.

Ferrari no. 56. Type 365 GTB 4, category GTS (chassis no. 16407), entered by North American Racing Team, driven by Ethuin and Guitteny. It came in 11th on distance, covering 3891.532km (2418.086 miles) at an average 162.147km/h (100.753mph).

Ethuin lost a lot of time with a brake problem, which meant going all out at Mulsanne. It should be noted tha this team was in 46th place at the end of the first hour.

Ferrari no. 57. Type 365 GTB 4, category GTS (chassis no. 13367), entered by Marvel Mignot, driven by Mignot and Jones. It was placed 16th on distance, covering 3638.968km (2261.150 miles) at an average 151.623km/h (94.214mph).

Ferrari no. 18. Type Dino 308 GT, Sports (Group 5) (chassis no. 08020), entered by North American Racing Team, driven by Lafosse and Gagliardi. It retired in the fourth hour, after occupying 38th place in the preceding hour.
This was the first outing for a Dino 308 at Le Mans – spoiled by gearbox damage.

Ferrari no. 55. Type 365 GTB 4, category GTS, entered by North American Racing Team, driven by Paoli and Couderc. It went out in the second hour, after being logged in 47th position in the preceding hour. Paoli ran into the barrier and had to retire.

1975

Two Ferraris start, two finish

At no time since the arrival of the marque at Le Mans in 1949 had such a thin representation of the red cars been seen. Luigi Chinetti, convinced that the four cars he was entering were going to qualify, cut practice short in order to economize on men and material. Too soon, it seemed – a Porsche stole a march on the Dino so that the latter did not in fact qualify. Chinetti dug in his heels to the point of having his Dino pushed to the starting line at 4pm on the Saturday. The ACO obviously refused to let it start; this put Chinetti into a towering rage, causing him to withdraw his other three cars.

The winners were Ickx and Bell in their Gulf Ford, with a distance of 4595.577km (2855.559 miles) at an average 191.482km/h (118.981mph).

Ferrari no. 47. Type 365 GTB 4, category GTS (chassis no. 16717), entered by Ecurie Francorchamps, driven by de Fierlant, Andruet and Pilette. It was in 12th place on distance, covering 4002.404km (2486.979 miles) at an average 166.766km/h (103.624mph).

The two 365 GTB 4 Daytonas found themselves alone at the start of the race against 15 Porsche Carreras. A ravenous appetite characterized the advance of this yelow and red car, which succeeded in hoisting itself into eighth place in the ninth hour. Unfortunately it was pushed back by the troubles it experienced (fuel consumption and an electrical short). However, it achieved a better placing than the other Ferrari and – a further reason for pride – it managed to pass the 4000km (2500-mile) mark, or 293 laps. In practice Andruet had achieved 4′ 24.3sec (the 35th time), which was an average for the circuit of 185.789km/h (115.444mph).

Ferrari no. 48. Type 365 GTB 4, category GTS (chassis no. 13367), entered by Marcel Mignot, driven by Mignot, Jones and Gurdjian. It came 13th on distance, covering 3997.871km (2484.162 miles) at an average 166.577km/h (103.506mph).

This Daytona conceded 4633m (5067yd) to the Ferrari in front. The midnight blue GTB suffered from low oil pressure and a loss of power that did not allow its drivers to press the advantage of its speed. It should be remembered that this was a chassis that was already old, fitted with a new engine since its American campaign. Its performance in practice was good: Mignot achieved 29th best time, 4′ 20.1sec, which represents a speed of 188.789km (117.308mph).

Ferrari no. 45. Type 365 GTB 4, category GTS (chassis no. 16407), entered by North American Racing Team, driven by Bucknum and Facetti.

This 1972 Daytona was scratched despite an excellent time in practice. Pacetti did 4′17.3sec – 190.843km/h (118.584mph) – which put it among the best of the GTS cars.

Ferrari no. 46. Type 365 GTB 4-NART, category GTX (chassis no. 15965), entered by North American Racing Team, driven by Malcher and Langlois.

In practice Malcher did a lap of 4′31.8sec – 180.662km/h (112.258mph) – in this Daytona Special with a Michelotti body. Like the other two NART Ferraris that succeeded in qualifying, it scratched.

Ferrari no. 17. Type Dino 308 GT 4, entered by North American Racing Team, driven by Gagliardi and Cluxton.

In practice Gagliardi clocked 4′32.9sec – 179.934km/h (111.806mph) – an acceptable time that Luigi Chinetti himself judged satisfactory. This, however, was a little premature because Wicky forced his Porsche to a better time than the Dino at full stretch. Chinetti's resulting wrath led him to withdraw his other three cars when number 17 was not permitted to start.

Ferrari no. 99. Type 365 GT/4BB, category GTX (chassis no. 18095), entered by North American Racing Team, driven by Guitteny and Haran.

Destined to contend for the IMSA championship this BB, the first to line up at the Le Mans start, was almost a production model and developed only 380bhp. Its performance at its first Transatlantic outings (Daytona, then Sebring) was hardly brilliant, then it came back across the Atlantic to take part in the Le Mans 24 Hours, where Guitteny clocked the best practice time of the non-homologated GT cars (4′30sec) – this represented 181.867km/h (113.007mph). Unfortunately Chinetti withdrew all his cars and the first BB at Le Mans was scratched.

1977

One Ferrari starts, one finishes

Once again there was victory for Porsche at Le Mans, the fourth and not the last. The expected Renault–Porsche duel, despite a more numerous entry from the French side, went in favour of the Germans after a real rout of the Renault prototypes. As for 1976, it should be pointed out that no Ferrari took part at Le Mans that year.

The 1977 winners were Barth, Haywood and Ickx in a Porsche 936, with 4671.630km (2902.816 miles) at an average speed of 194.651km/h (120.951mph).

Ferrari no. 75. Type 365 GTB 4, IMSA (chassis no. 18095), entered by North American Racing Team, driven by Migault, Guitteny and 'Cocholopez'. It was placed 16th on distance, covering 3667.640km (2278.966 miles) at an average 152.818km/h (94.957mph).
A class victory for this old Ferrari, modified with enlarged wings and Naca, which finished also in fifth place in the IMSA category. The sole Ferrari came in just ahead of the sole Aston Martin entered. Times had certainly changed when you consider how these two marques had formerly shone, up among the winners. This BB achieved an average speed better by 20km/h (12mph) than that clocked by the winning 166 MM in 1949.

1978

Five Ferraris start, one finishes

The great Renault–Porsche contest had its dénouement in this year's Le Mans 24 Hours: after Talbot in 1950, Matra in 1972, 1973, and 1974, a third French marque inscribed its name on the list of winners.

Ferrari, after drawing the crowds to the grandstands and, as it were, the terraces, was only a shadow of its former self, getting only one car to the finish.

The winning team were Pitoni and Jaussaud in their Renault Alpine A442B, at an average speed of 210.188km/h (130.605mph) over 5044.530km (3134.526 miles).

Ferrari no. 86. Type 365 GT 4B, IMSA (chassis no. 18095), entered by Grand Competition Cars, driven by Migault and Guitteny. It finished in 16th place on distance, covering 3579.340km (2224.099 miles) at an average 149.139km/h (92.671mph).

This was the survivor among the Ferraris. Of the five entered it had, with Guitteny at the wheel, recorded the poorest time in practice at 4'15.9sec. Serious gearbox problems involving its replacement occurred after an hour and a half of the race. Forty nine minutes were lost in these repairs – which did not prevent a second stop at 17 minutes before midnight. From being in fifth place in the third hour it ended up lying in 16th in the 17th hour, overtaking one Porsche. In addition it took third place in the IMSA category and completed 262 laps.

Ferrari no. 85. Type 512 BB, IMSA (chassis no. 22715), entered by Jean 'Beurlys', driven by Pilette, 'Beurlys' and Touroul. It retired at 6.57pm, after being in 46th place in the preceding hour.

A very short race for this BB, which in fact was driven only by Teddy Pilette. The worn transmission gave out when Raymond Touroul took over from the Belgian. The latter had recorded 4'10.9sec in practice, which put the car on the 21st spot of the grid.

Ferrari no. 89. Type 512 BB, IMSA, entered by C. Pozzi, Thomson and JMS Racing, driven by Ballot, Léna and Lafosse. It retired at 9.10am, after being in 12th position in the preceding hour.

Ballot and Léna had the best time of the Ferraris in practice with 4'07.1sec, putting the car on the 17th line at the start. With this car, too, it was the transmission that forced its withdrawal on the Sunday morning.

Ferrari no. 88. Type 512 BB, IMSA, entered by C. Pozzi, Thomson and JMS Racing, driven by Andruet and Dini. It retired at 12.07pm, after being in 13th place in the preceding hour. In practice Andruet had clocked the second-best time of the Ferraris, with 4'07.3sec, which put the car on the 17th line.

After three hours of the race the clutch cost this team 40 minutes, then other problems – the carburettor and the fuel pump – added several minutes' more delay. Finally it was the transmission that prevented this French BB from continuing an event in which its best placing had been 11th.

Ferrari no. 87. Type 512 BB, IMSA, entered by North American Racing Team, driven by Guérin, Delaunay and Young. It retired at 9.38am, after being in 11th place in the preceding hour. Guérin qualified the car with 4'16.3sec, putting it on the 18th line at the start. The gearbox cost the team 17 minutes in the night. The withdrawal of this car came after it had been in second place in its group for some time.

1979

Four Ferraris start, one finishes

A fifth Porsche victory at the Le Mans 24 Hours – but not by the expected car.

A 935 from a private team played the role of the North American Racing Team LM in 1965, walking off with the coveted victory. Renault, despite its success the previous year, did not deem it advantageous to return to Le Mans. So it was the team of Ludwig and Bill and Don Whittington in the Porsche 935 K3 who won at an average 173.914km/h (108.065mph) over 4173.930km (1593.560 miles).

Ferrari no. 61. Type 512 BB, IMSA (chassis no. 27577), entered by Jean 'Beurlys', driven by Dryver, Faure, O'Rourke and 'Beurlys'. It finished in 12th place on distance, covering 3668.362km (2279.414 miles) at an average 152.848km/h (94.875mph).
This was the only surviving Ferrari. It had, however, recorded the worst time of the Ferraris in practice, with 4′11.98sec set by Faure. After experiencing difficulties because of the wet surface, and some minor but nonetheless embarrassing problems, this Belgian Ferrari crossed the finishing line with Jean Blaton, alias 'Beurlys' at the wheel, celebrating his 15th Le Mans 24 Hours. This car completed 269 laps, putting itself in fifth place in the IMSA category. Its best position overall was 11th, in the 17th and 18th hours.

Ferrari no. 62. Type 512 BB, IMSA (chassis no. 26681), entered by C. Pozzi and JMS Racing, driven by Andruet and Dini. It retired at 9.25am, after being in eighth place in the preceding hour.

Andruet made the second best time in practice (4'02.42sec) of the Ferraris entered. During the race Jean-Claude did more of the driving than his partner and had to put up with a badly fixed dashboard. His best position was sixth, which he held in the 19th hour. This BB, like number 63, was prepared at Maranello.

Ferrari no. 63. Type 512 BB, IMSA (chassis no. 26685), entered by C. Pozzi and JMS Racing, driven by Ballot, Léna, Leclère and Gregg. It went out at 7.53am, after being in 10th place in the preceding hour: Michel Leclère, then at the wheel, collided with car number 33, the Chevron B 36 Roc de Tarres, at Post 70 on the Hunaudières. This driver had clocked the best time of the Ferraris in practice: 4'00.78sec.

The bodies of the new BBs had been worked on in the Pininfarina wind tunnel where they had gained in refinement, and also size, but were heavier by some 30kg (66lb).

Ferrari no. 64. Type 512 BB, IMSA (chassis no. 26683), entered by North American Racing Team, driven by Delaunay, Henn and Grandet. It retired at 6.04pm, after being in 47th position in the preceding hour. Preston Henn went off the road at Post 18 on the Tertre-Rouge bend.

In practice Delaunay had achieved 4'06.3sec. The pneumatic jacks fitted to BBs made their first appearance on this car.

Captions to coloured illustrations

Page 129: *(above) Olivier Gendebien at the wheel of his Ferrari 250 TR in 1959. (below) The California spyder that came fifth that same year.*

Page 130: *(above) 250 GT of the Ecurie Francorchamps, the first Ferrari placed in 1959. (centre) Tavano's 250 GT in 1960. (below) The 250 TR1 of the Rodriguez brothers in 1961.*

Page 131: *The 'Eldé' and 'Beurlys' GTO in 1962.*

Page 132: *Pierre Noblet's GTO in 1962.*

Page 133: *(above) The Belgian national team's GTO in 1963. (below) The 1965 Ferrari 365 P2 with Vaccarella at the wheel.*

Page 134: *(from top to bottom) The 1966 Dino 206 SP entered by North American Racing Team and the Belgian 250 LM.*

Pages 136 and 137: *(above) The unforgettable P4s of 1967.*

Page 137: *(below) In 1970 two Ferrari 512 Ss of the Scuderia Filipinetti and Page 138 (above) a 1971 512 M belonging to the same team. (below) Mark Donohue's famous 512 M, 1971.*

Page 139: *(above) The Posey-Adamovicz 365 GTB 4 Daytona in 1972. (below) The three official 312PBs, 1973 and the 1972 NART Dino.*

Page 140: *(above) The Grandet-Bardini Daytona, victorious in the GT category, 1974. (centre) The Dino 308 GT and the 312 P of the same year. (below) The first Boxer to finish at Le Mans, 1977.*

Pages 141 to 144: *Variations on the Ferrari Boxer theme, 1977 to 1984.*

1980

Five Ferraris start, two finish

A surprise victory for Rondeau in the Le Mans 24 Hours. This result was all the more congenial for being a case of David bringing down Goliath: the nice, straightforward kind of plot that has always pleased the Le Mans public. For the first time in the history of the event a driver-constructor won it in his own car. Rondeau and Jaussaud did 4608.202km (2863.291 miles) at an average 192.000km/h (119.303mph). in their Rondeau M379 B.

Ferrari no. 76. Type 512 BB, IMSA (chassis no.32129), entered by C. Pozzi and JMS Racing, driven by Dieudonné, Xhenceval and Regout. It finished in 10th place on distance, covering 4257.097km (2645.237 miles) at an average 177.379km/h (110.218mph).
In spite of his new lightened chassis, Dieudonné was not able to get below the 4-minute mark for the circuit in practice (4′05.1sec). Intelligent and consistent driving took this Ferrari forward from 43rd to 10th place, despite a slight bump that necessitated a quick repair to the bodywork. The car achieved a speed of 328km/h (204mph) at 7500 rpm on the Hunaudières straight. By the finish it had covered 312 laps and was in third place in the IMSA category.

Ferrari no. 78. Type 512 BB, IMSA (chassis no. 27577), entered by EMKA Productions Ltd, driven by O'Rourke, Down and Philipps. It came 23rd in the distance placings, covering 3581.522km (2225.455 miles) at an average 149.230km/h (92.727mph).

This was the miracle of Le Mans. After indifferent practice times (4′14sec), the best time made by O'Rourke, this BB was in first reserve position and benefited from the scratching of the NART Ferrari. Starting in 56th position this green Ferrari, which, painted yellow, had already taken part at Le Mans in 1979, finished the event with red panels over its rear – spare parts from the Bellancauto BB. After 37 pit stops caused by numerous problems (from the spark plugs to the floor pan dragging on the ground), this brave team finished 23rd overall and eighth in its class.

Ferrari no. 77. Type 512 BB, IMSA (chassis no. 31589), entered by C. Pozzi and JMS Racing, driven by Andruet, Ballot and Léna. It retired at 3.25am, after being in 27th position in the preceding hour. In practice it had achieved the best lap time of the five Ferraris entered – 3′57.9sec, with Andruet at the wheel.

This new 1980 BB was fitted with the new chassis LM, lightened by almost 100kg (220lb). The body too had been improved; the most important modification was that the sides were now vertical. The engine rated close on 470bhp and fuel consumption varied between 40 and 45 litres/100km. Like the other BB LMs the Ballot-Léna car was inadequately sealed under the engine and let in the water that was flooding the track, and this affected the ignition. It was the best-placed Ferrari (15th) when it retired – officially with engine failure.

Ferrari no. 75. Type 512 BB, IMSA(chassis no. 26685), entered by C. Pozzi and JMS Racing, driven by Guitteny, Bleynie and Libert. It retired in the seventh hour, after being in 45th place in the preceding hour.

The Belgian Paul Libert was a student at the European University in Antwerp. For his end-of-studies thesis he started a project entitled *Fondation Le Mans*. The aim to run three Ferraris at Le Mans. He collected funds, Jean Graton (alias Michel Vaillant) decorated the cars and he negotiated an agreement with Pozzi and JMS. In short, after a great deal of effort and imagination, three BBs lined up at the start of the 1980 Le Mans.

The number 75 Ferrari had already competed at Le Mans in 1979 and had been little modified since. Guitteny did a 4′06.8sec lap in practice but, in the event itself, Bleynie went off the road at Post 19 and retired, depriving Libert of the pleasure of driving the BB in the race.

Ferrari no. 79. Type 512 BB, IMSA (chassis no. 28601), entered by Scuderia Supercar Bellancauto, driven by Dini, Violati and Michelangeli. It went out at 5.18pm, after lying in 35th position in the preceding hour. This was the first Ferrari to retire, after only 1 hour 18 minutes of the race. Spartaco Dini shot off the road in the new section of the circuit and damaged the car too badly for any hope of continuing. Only the rear body cover reached the finish – on loan to the British Ferrari, number 78.

Ferrari no. 74. Type 512 BB, IMSA (chassis no. 30599), entered by North American Racing Team, driven by Henn and Delaunay.

This car did not start: Luigi Chinetti scratched as the engine had seized in practice with a lubrication problem. The car was fitted with Porsche 935 brakes, which made possible practice lap time of 4′11.2sec. The withdrawal of this car was obviously to the advantage of number 78, the British-entered Ferrari.

1981

Five Ferraris start, two finish

A sixth victory for Porsche in the Le Mans 24 Hours, and a return for Ferrari who placed a 512 BB in fifth position, winning the IGTX category.

The winners overall were Ickx and Bell in the Porsche 936/81 with 4825.348km (2998.332 miles) at an average 201.056km/h (124.930mph).

Ferrari no. 47. Type 512 BB, IMSA-GTX (chassis no. 31589; engine no. 023), entered by C. Pozzi, driven by Andruet, Ballot and Léna. It finished fifth on distance, covering 4469.433km (2777.177 miles) at an average 186.226km/h (115.715mph).

This car, with a not altogether satisfactory engine, came last but one of the Ferraris in practice (Ballot and Léna with 3'56.89sec). The mechanics had to change the engine and the gearbox before the start. Wisely, this Ferrari entered by the French importer ran a little behind the American BB from NART. The Frenchmen nevertheless finished in an excellent fifth place overall and first in their group. It should be pointed out that this was the best performance by a BB at Le Mans.

Ferrari no. 46. Type 512 BB, IMSA-GTX (chassis no. 35525; engine no. 021), entered by Rennod Racing, driven by Dieudonné, Xhenceval and Libert. It was ninth on distance, covering 4370.941km (2715.977 miles) at an average 182.122km/h (113.165mph).

The car would have done even better if Dieudonné, who became ill had not had to leave the driving to his team mates (he only did four hours, Libert six and Xhenceval 14). In practice Dieudonné had had the third-best time with 3'56.72sec. This car completed 320 laps, finishing third in its group after a very regular run without any particular alarms.

Ferrari no. 45. Type 512 BBB, IMSA-GTX (chassis no. 28601), entered by Scuderia Supercar Bellancauto, driven by Violati, Flammini and Truffo. It retired at 5.03am, after lying in 20th place in the preceding hour.

Despite its elongated, tapering form, given it by the engineer Armando Pallanca, this BBB (Berlina Boxer Bellancauto) was the slowest on the Hunaudières straight. In practice Flammini had done 3'55.66sec, putting the car in second place with the best time of the five Ferraris entered. Unfortunately it had electrical problems, then trouble with the injection pump, which held it back. These difficulties re-emerged during the night, forcing it to give up after completing 118 laps.

Ferrari no. 49. Type 512 BB, IMSA-GTX (chassis no. 35527; engine no. 025), entered by North American Racing Team, driven by Cudini, Gurdjian and Morton. It went out at 9.45am, after being in 15th place in the preceding hour.

With Cudini driving, the car had taken pole position among the Ferraris (with 3'52.6sec) and set off in great style, getting into fourth place overall and staying there for several hours. Philippe Gurdjian left the road at 9.12am, forcing retirement of the car at Post 125.

Ferrari no. 48. Type 512 BB, IMSA-GTX (chassis no. 35523; engine no. 020), entered by Simon Phillips, driven by Phillips, Salmon and Earle. It retired at 2.25am, after being in 19th position in the preceding hour.

This was the worst of the Ferraris in practice, with Michel Salmon doing a 4'02.75sec lap. This smart white British-entered Ferrari had to change its radiator, then gave up with a twisted chassis in the night after completing 140 laps. Its best placing had been 19th.

1982

Four Ferraris start, two finish

The seventh victory in the Le Mans 24 Hours for Porsche, which was progressing towards the record of nine wins held by Ferrari.

The winners were Ickx and Bell who in their Porsche 956 T did 4899.086km (3044.151 miles) at an average 204.128km/h (126.839mph).

Ferrari no. 70. Type 512 BB, IMSA-GTX, entered by Prancing Horse Farm Racing, driven by Dieudonné, Baird and Libert. It finished sixth on distance, covering 4387.786km (2726.444 miles) at an average 182.824km/h (113.602mph).

The first of the Ferraris to qualify after the Cudini retirement, this car took third place in the IMSA-GTX category, behind two Porsche 935s. Earlier troubles, and changing the fuel pump, had held it back. In practice Dieudonné had had the second-best time of the four Ferraris with 3′56.52sec.

Ferrari no. 71. Type 512 BB, IMSA-GTX, entered by Pozzi-Ferrari France, driven by Andruet, Ballot, Léna and Regout. It retired at 8.20pm, after lying in 37th place in the preceding hour.

During practice the car's oil pressure was already tending to drop and it would have been wise to change the engine. This was not done and very soon the car had to retire with engine failure. In practice, with Ballot driving, it had had the third-best time of the four Ferraris: 3′56.8sec.

Ferrari no. 73. Type 512 BB, IMSA/GTX, entered by T-Bird Swap Shop, driven by Henn, Lanier and Morin. It retired at 7.25pm, after occupying 44th place in the preceding hour, with engine trouble. It had clocked the worst time of the Ferraris: 4′07.32sec, with Henn.

Ferrari no. 72. Type 512 BB, IMSA-GTX, entered by North American Racing Team, driven by Cudini, Morton and Paul. It finished ninth on distance, covering 4182.783km (2599.061 miles) at an average 174.282km/h (108.294mph).
Cudini had the best time of the four Ferraris in practice with 3′54.07sec. After completing 306 laps of Le Mans, the car took fourth in its group.

1984

One Ferrari starts, none finish

The ninth victory for Porsche in the Le Mans 24 Hours. The German firm had equalled the Ferrari record. By way of making the Le Mans crowd still more nostalgic, a solitary 512 BB was entered for the event; it did somewhat less than brilliantly.

The winning team were Pescarolo and Ludwig in their Porsche 956 T at an average of 204.178km/h (126.870mph) for 4900.276km (3044.890 miles). Well done Henri; till the next time Ferrari!

Ferrari no. 27. Type 512 BB, GTX (chassis no. 35529), entered by SC Supercar Bellancauto, driven by Michangeli, Marazzi and Lacaud. It retired in the eighth hour, after being in 43rd position in the preceding hour.

It was Marazzi who secured the best qualifying time, 4'00.2sec, during the second round of practice (this represents a lap at an average speed of 204.219km/h or 126.896mph). After starting on the 22nd line of the grid, the only Ferrari in the 1984 Le Mans was in 36th place at the end of the first hour. At 8.55pm it retired officially at Arnage: the reason was gearbox trouble. Earlier this Ferrari Boxer had been timed at 307km/h (191mph) on the Hunaudières straight. It had completed 65 laps before having to give up, a distance of 886km (551 miles).

TECHNICAL INFORMATION ON THE FERRARIS AT LE MANS

1949

Race no.	Type	Engine position	No. of cyls & configur.	Capacity in cc	Bore & stroke/mm	Carburation	Ignition	Tyres	Brakes	Gearbox	Body material	Weight in kg
22	166 MM	front	V12	1995	60 × 58.8	3 carb.	magneto	Pirelli	Drums	Ferrari 4 + rev.	aluminium	
23	166 MM	front	V12	1995	60 × 58.8	3 carb.	magneto	Pirelli	Drums	Ferrari 4 + rev.	aluminium	

1950

Race no.	Type	Engine position	No. of cyls & configur.	Capacity in cc	Bore & stroke/mm	Carburation	Ignition	Tyres	Brakes	Gearbox	Body material	Weight in kg
24	195 SB	front	V12	2341	65 × 58.8	1 carb.	magneto		drum	Ferrari 4 + rev.	aluminium	
25	195 SC	front	V12	2341	65 × 58.8	1 carb.	mageneto		drum	Ferrari 4 + rev.	aluminium	
26	166 MMB	front	V12	1995	60 × 58.8	3 carb.	magneto		drum	Ferrari 4 + rev	aluminium	
27	166 MMC	front	V12	1995	60 × 58.8	3 carb.	magneto		drum	Ferrari 4 + rev	aluminium	
28	166 MM	front	V12	1995	60 × 58.8	3 carb.	magneto		drum	Ferrari 4 + rev.	aluminium	

1951

Race no.	Type	Engine position	No. of cyls & configur.	Capacity in cc	Bore & stroke/mm	Carburation	Ignition	Tyres	Brakes	Gearbox	Body material	Weight in kg
15	340 America	front	V12	4102		3 Weber	distrib.		4 drum	Ferrari 4 + rev.	aluminium	
16	340 America	front	V12	4102		3 Weber	distrib.		4 drum	Ferrari 4 + rev.	aluminium	
17	340 America	front	V12	4102		3 Weber	distrib.		4 drum	Ferrari 4 + rev.	aluminium	
18	340 America	front	V12	4102		3 Weber	distrib.		4 drum	Ferrari 4 + rev.	aluminium	
29	212 Export	front	V12	2563	68 × 58.8		magneto		4 drum	Ferrari 4 + rev.	aluminium	
30	212 Export	front	V12	2563	68 × 58.8		magneto		4 drum	Ferrari 4 + rev.	aluminium	
31	212 Export	front	V12	2563	68 × 58.8		magento		4 drum	Ferrari 4 + rev.	aluminium	
32	166 MM	front	V12	1995	60 × 58.8	3 Weber	magneto		4 drum	Ferrari 4 + rev.	aluminium	
64	166 MM	front	V12	1995	60 × 58.8	3 Weber	magneto		4 drum	Ferrari 4 + rev.	aluminium	

1952

Race no.	Type	Engine position	No. of cyls & configur.	Capacity in cc	Bore & stroke/mm	Carburation	Ignition	Tyres	Brakes	Gearbox	Body material	Weight in kg
12	340 America	front	V12	4102		3 Weber	distrib.		4 drum	Ferrari 4 + rev.	aluminium	
14	340 America	front	V12	4102		3 Weber	distrib.		4 drum	Ferrari 4 + rev.	aluminium	
15	340 America	front	V12	4102		3 Weber	distrib.		4 drum	Ferrari 4 + rev.	aluminium	
16	340 America	front	V12	4102		3 Weber	distrib.		4 drum	Ferrari 4 + rev.	aluminium	
30	225 S	front	V12	2715	70 × 58.8	3 Weber	distrib.		4 drum	Ferrari 4 + rev.	aluminium	
33	212 Export	front	V12	2562	68 × 58.8	3 Weber	distrib.		4 drum	Ferrari 4 + rev.	aluminium	
62	250 S	front	V12	2953	73 × 58.8	3 Weber	distrib.		4 drum	Ferrari 4 + rev.	aluminium	

1953

Race no.	Type	Engine position	No. of cyls & configur.	Capacity in cc	Bore & stroke/mm	Carburation	Ignition	Tyres	Brakes	Gearbox	Body material	Weight in kg
12	340 MM	front	V12	4494	80 × 74.5	3 carb.	Marelli		4 drum	Ferrari 4 + rev.	aluminium	
14	340 MM	front	V12	4102	80 × 68	3 carb.	Marelli		4 drum	Ferrari 4 + rev.	aluminium	
15	340 MM	front	V12	4102	80 × 68	3 carb.	Marelli		4 drum	Ferrari 4 + rev.	aluminium	
16	340 MM	front	V12	4102	80 × 68	3 carb.	Marelli		4 drum	Ferrari 4 + rev.	aluminium	

1954

Race no.	Type	Engine position	No. of cyls & configur.	Capacity in cc	Bore & stroke/mm	Carburation	Ignition	Tyres	Brakes	Gearbox	Body material	Weight in kg
3	375 plus	front	V12	4954	84 × 74.5	3 Weber	delco Marelli	Pirelli	4 drum	Ferrari 4 + rev.	aluminium	
4	375 plus	front	V12	4954	84 × 74.5	3 Weber	delco Marelli	Pirelli	4 drum	Ferrari 4 + rev.	aluminium	approx 1400
5	375 plus	front	V12	4954	84 × 74.5	3 Weber	delco Marelli	Pirelli	4 drum	Ferrari 4 + rev.	aluminium	
6	C 375 MM	front	V12	4522	84 × 68	3 Weber	delco Marelli	Firestone	4 drum	Ferrari 4 + rev.	aluminium	approx 1350
18	375 MM	front	V12	4522	84 × 68	3 Weber	delco Marelli	Pirelli	4 drum	Ferrari 4 + rev.	aluminium	approx 1400

1955

Race no.	Type	Engine position	No. of cyls & configur.	Capacity in cc	Bore & stroke/mm	Carburation	Ignition	Tyres	Brakes	Gearbox	Body material	Weight in kg
3	735 LM	front	6	4412	102 × 90	3 Weber	delco Marelli	Englebert	4 drum	Ferrari 4 + rev.	aluminium	
4	735 LM	front	6	4412	102 × 90	3 Weber	delco Marelli	Englebert	4 drum	Ferrari 4 + rev.	aluminium	
5	735 LM	front	6	4412	102 × 90	3 Weber	delco Marelli	Englebert	4 drum	Ferrari 4 + rev.	aluminium	
12	750 M	front	4	2999	103 × 90	2 Weber	delco Marelli	Dunlop	4 drum	Ferrari 4 + rev.	aluminium	
14	750 M	front	4	2999	103 × 90	2 Weber	delco Marelli	Dunlop	4 drum	Ferrari 4 + rev.	aluminium	

1956

Race no.	Type	Engine position	No. of cyls & configur.	Capacity in cc	Bore & stroke/mm	Carburation	Ignition	Tyres	Brakes	Gearbox	Body material	Weight in kg
10	625 LM	front	4	2498	94 × 90	2 Weber	Marelli	Englebert	4 drum	Ferrari 4 + rev.	aluminium	
11	625 LM	front	4	2498	94 × 90	2 Weber	Marelli	Englebert	4 drum	Ferrari 4 + rev.	aluminium	
12	625 LM	front	4	2498	94 × 90	2 Weber	Marelli	Englebert	4 drum	Ferrari 4 + rev.	aluminium	
20	500 TR	front	4	1984	90 × 78	2 Weber	Marelli	Englebert	4 drum	Ferrari 4 + rev.	aluminium	
21	500 TR	front	4	1984	90 × 78	2 Weber	Marelli	Dunlop	4 drum	Ferrari 4 + rev.	aluminium	
22	500 TR	front	4	1984	90 × 78	2 Weber	Marelli	Englebert	4 drum	Ferrari 4 + rev.	aluminium	

The start of the 1956 Le Mans 24 Hours.

1957

Race no.	Type	Engine position	No. of cyls & configur.	Capacity in cc	Bore & stroke/mm	Carburation	Ignition	Tyres	Brakes	Gearbox	Body material	Weight in kg
6	335 S	front	V12	4023	77 × 72	3 Solex	Marelli	Englebert	4 drum	Ferrari 4 + rev.	aluminium	
7	335 S	front	V12	4023	77 × 72	3 Solex	Marelli	Englebert	4 drum	Ferrari 4 + rev.	aluminium	
8	315 S	front	V12	3783	76 × 69.5	3 Solex	Marelli	Englebert	4 drum	Ferrari 4 + rev.	aluminium	
9	250 TR	front	V12	3117	75 × 58.5	3 Solex	Marelli	Englebert	4 drum	Ferrari 4 + rev.	aluminium	
10	290 MM	front	V12	3490	73 × 69.5	3 Weber	Marelli	Englebert	4 drum	Ferrari 4 + rev.	aluminium	
11	290 MM	front	V12	3490	73 × 69.5	3 Weber	Marelli	Englebert	4 drum	Ferrari 4 + rev.	aluminium	
27	500 TR	front	in-line 4	1985	90 × 78	2 Weber	Marelli	Englebert	4 drum	Ferrari 4 + rev.	aluminium	
28	500 TR	front	in-line 4	1985	90 × 78	2 Weber	Marelli	Englebert	4 drum	Ferrari 4 + rev.	aluminium	
29	500 TR	front	in-line 4	1985	90 × 78	2 Weber	Marelli	Englebert	4 drum	Ferrari 4 + rev.	aluminium	
61	500 TR	front	in-line 4	1985	90 × 78	2 Weber	Marelli	Pirelli	4 drum	Ferrari 4 + rev.	aluminium	

1958

Race no.	Type	Engine position	No. of cyls & configur.	Capacity in cc	Bore & stroke/mm	Carburation	Ignition	Tyres	Brakes	Gearbox	Body material	Weight in kg
12	250 TR	front	V12	2953	73 × 58.8	6 Weber	Marelli	Englebert	4 drum	Ferrari 4 + rev.	aluminium	
14	250 TR	front	V12	2953	73 × 58.8	6 Weber	Marelli	Englebert	4 drum	Ferrari 4 + rev.	aluminium	
16	250 TR	front	V12	2953	73 × 58.8	6 Weber	Marelli	Englebert	4 drum	Ferrari 4 + rev.	aluminium	
17	250 TR	front	V12	2953	73 × 58.8	6 Weber	Marelli	Englebert	4 drum	Ferrari 4 + rev.	aluminium	
18	250 TR	front	V12	2953	73 × 58.8	6 Weber	Marelli	Englebert	4 drum	Ferrari 4 + rev.	aluminium	
19	250 TR	front	V12	2953	73 × 58.8	6 Weber	Marelli	Englebert	4 drum	Ferrari 4 + rev.	aluminium	
20	250 TR	front	V12	2953	73 × 58.8	6 Weber	Marelli	Englebert	4 drum	Ferrari 4 + rev.	aluminium	
21	250 TR	front	V12	2953	73 × 58.8	6 Weber	Marelli	Dunlop	4 drum	Ferrari 4 + rev.	aluminium	
22	250 TR	front	V12	2953	73 × 58.8	6 Weber	Marelli	Firestone	4 drum	Ferrari 4 + rev.	aluminium	
25	500 TR	front	in-line 4	1985	90 × 78	2 Weber	Marelli	Englebert	4 drum	Ferrari 4 + rev.	aluminium	
58	500 TR	front	V12	2953	73 × 58.8	6 Weber	Marelli	Dunlop	4 drum	Ferrari 4 + rev.	aluminium	

1959

Race no.	Type	Engine position	No. of cyls & configur.	Capacity in cc	Bore & stroke/mm	Carburation	Ignition	Tyres	Brakes	Gearbox	Body material	Weight in kg
10	250 TR/58	front	V12	2953	73 × 58.8	6 Weber	Marelli	Dunlop	4 disc	Ferrari 4 + rev.	aluminium	800
11	250 GT	front	V12	2953	73 × 58.8	3 Weber	Marelli	Dunlop	4 disc	Ferrari 4 + rev.	aluminium	
12	250 TR/59	front	V12	2953	73 × 58.8	6 Weber	Marelli	Dunlop	4 disc	Ferrari 5 + rev.	aluminium	
14	250 TR/59	front	V12	2953	73 × 58.8	6 Weber	Marelli	Dunlop	4 disc	Ferrari 5 + rev.	aluminium	
15	250 TR/59	front	V12	2953	73 × 58.8	6 Weber	Marelli	Dunlop	4 disc	Ferrari 5 + rev.	aluminium	
16	250 GT	front	V12	2953	73 × 58.8	3 Weber	Marelli	Englebert	4 disc	Ferrari 4 + rev.	aluminium	
17	250 TR	front	V12	2953	73 × 58.8	6 Weber	Marelli	Dunlop	4 disc	Ferrari 5 + rev.	aluminium	
18	250 GT	front	V12	2953	73 × 58.8	3 Weber	Marelli	Dunlop	4 disc	Ferrari 4 + rev.	aluminium	
19	250 TR/58	front	V12	2953	73 × 58.8	6 Weber	Marelli	Goodyear	4 disc	Ferrari 4 + rev.	aluminium	
20	250 GT	front	V12	2953	73 × 58.8	3 Weber	Marelli	Dunlop	4 disc	Ferrari 4 + rev.	aluminium	900
23	Dino 196 S	front	V6	1983	77 × 71	3 Weber	Marelli	Dunlop	4 disc	Ferrari 4 + rev.	aluminium	

1960

Race no.	Type	Engine position	No. of cyls & configur.	Capacity in cc	Bore & stroke/mm	Carburation	Ignition	Tyres	Brakes	Gearbox	Body material	Weight in kg
9	TRI/60	front	V12	2953	73 × 58.8	6 Weber	Marelli	Dunlop	4 disc	Ferrari 6 + rev.	aluminium	768
10	TR/60	front	V12	2953	73 × 58.8	6 Weber	Marelli	Dunlop	4 disc	Ferrari 6 + rev.	aluminium	830
11	TR/60	front	V12	2953	73 × 58.8	6 Weber	Marelli	Dunlop	4 disc	Ferrari 6 + rev.	aluminium	830
12	TRI/60	front	V12	2953	73 × 58.8	6 Weber	Marelli	Dunlop	4 disc	Ferrari 6 + rev.	aluminium	768
15	250 GT	front	V12	2953	73 × 58.8	3 Weber	Marelli	Dunlop	4 disc	Ferrari 4 + rev.	aluminium	
16	250 GT	front	V12	2953	73 × 58.8	3 Weber	Marelli	Dunlop	4 disc	Ferrari 4 + rev.	aluminium	1170
17	250 TR	front	V12	2953	73 × 58.8	6 Weber	Marelli	Dunlop	4 disc	Ferrari 5 + rev.	aluminium	885
18	250 GT	front	V12	2953	73 × 58.8	3 Weber	Marelli	Dunlop	4 disc	Ferrari 4 + rev.	aluminium	1028
19	250 GT	front	V12	2953	73 × 58.8	3 Weber	Marelli	Dunlop	4 disc	Ferrari 4 + rev.	aluminium	1054
20	250 GT	front	V12	2953	73 × 58.8	3 Weber	Marelli	Dunlop	4 disc	Ferrari 4 + rev.	aluminium	1054
21	250 GT	front	V12	2953	73 × 58.8	3 Weber	Marelli	Dunlop	4 disc	Ferrari 4 + rev.	aluminium	1000
22	250 GT	front	V12	2953	73 × 58.8	3 Weber	Marelli	Dunlop	4 disc	Ferrari 4 + rev.	aluminium	1000

1961

Race no.	Type	Engine position	No. of cyls & configur.	Capacity in cc	Bore & stroke/mm	Carburation	Ignition	Tyres	Brakes	Gearbox	Body material	Weight in kg
10	TRI/61	front	V12	2953	73 × 58.8	6 Weber	Marelli	Dunlop	4 disc	Ferrari 5 + rev.	aluminium	
11	TRI/61	front	V12	2953	73 × 58.8	6 Weber	Marelli	Dunlop	4 disc	Ferrari 5 + rev.	aluminium	
12	250 GT Export	front	V12	2953	73 × 58.8	6 Weber	Marelli	Dunlop	4 disc	Ferrari 4 + rev.	aluminium	
14	250 GT	front	V12	2953	73 × 58.8	3 Weber	Marelli	Dunlop	4 disc	Ferrari 4 + rev.	aluminium	970
15	250 GT	front	V12	2953	73 × 58.8	3 Weber	Marelli	Dunlop	4 disc	Ferrari 4 + rev.	aluminium	950
16	250 GT	front	V12	2953	73 × 58.8	3 Weber	Marelli	Dunlop	4 disc	Ferrari 4 + rev.	aluminium	
17	TRI/61	front	V12	2953	73 × 58.8	6 Weber	Marelli	Dunlop	4 disc	Ferrari 5 + rev.	aluminium	
18	250 GT	front	V12	2953	73 × 58.8	3 Weber	Marelli	Dunlop	4 disc	Ferrari 4 + rev.	aluminium	
19	250 GT	front	V12	2953	73 × 58.8	3 Weber	Marelli	Dunlop	4 disc	Ferrari 4 + rev.	aluminium	
20	250 GT	front	V12	2953	73 × 58.8	3 Weber	Marelli	Dunlop	4 disc	Ferrari 4 + rev.	aluminium	970
23	246 SP	front	V6	2420	85 × 71	3 Weber	Marelli	Dunlop	4 disc	Ferrari 4 + rev.	aluminium	

The winning Ferrari at the finish, 1961.

1962

Race no.	Type	Engine position	No. of cyls & configur.	Capacity in cc	Bore & stroke/mm	Carburation	Ignition	Tyres	Brakes	Gearbox	Body material	Weight in kg
6	330 LM	front	V12	3967	77 × 71	6 Weber	Marelli	Dunlop	4 disc	Ferrari 5 + rev.	aluminium	
7	330 GT	front	V12	3967	77 × 71	6 Weber	Marelli	Dunlop	4 disc	Ferrari 5 + rev.	aluminium	
15	250 TRI	front	V12	2953	73 × 58.8	6 Weber	Marelli	Dunlop	4 disc	Ferrari 4 + rev.	aluminium	812
16	250 GT Breadvan	front	V12	2953	73 × 58.8	6 Weber	Marelli	Dunlop	4 disc	Ferrari 5 + rev.	aluminium	935
17	250 GTO	front	V12	2953	73 × 58.8	6 Weber	Marelli	Dunlop	4 disc	Ferrari 5 + rev.	aluminium	
18	250 TR/61	front	V12	2953	73 × 58.8	6 weber	Marelli	Goodyear	4 disc	Ferrari 5 + rev.	aluminium	835
19	250 GTO	front	V12	2953	73 × 58.8	6 Weber	Marelli	Dunlop	4 disc	Ferrari 5 + rev.	aluminium	1015
20	250 GTO	front	V12	2953	73 × 58.8	6 Weber	Marelli	Dunlop	4 disc	Ferrari 5 + rev.	aluminium	995
21	250 GT Export	front	V12	2953	73 × 58.8	6 Weber	Marelli	Dunlop	4 disc	Ferrari 4 + rev.	aluminium	995
22	250 GT	front	V12	2953	73 × 58.8	6 Weber	Marelli	Dunlop	4 disc	Ferrari 5 + rev.	aluminium	1010
23	250 GT	front	V12	2953	73 × 8.8	6 Weber	Marelli	Dunlop	4 disc	Ferrari 5 + rev.	aluminium	979
27	268 SP	rear	V8	2645		3 Weber	Marelli	Dunlop	4 disc	Ferrari 5 + rev.	aluminium	
28	246 SP	rear	V6	2420	85 × 71	3 Weber	Marelli	Dunlop	4 disc	Ferrari 5 + rev.	aluminium	
58	250 GTO	front	V12	2953	73 × 58.8	6 Weber	Marelli	Dunlop	4 disc	Ferrari 5 + rev.	aluminium	1000
59	250 GT	front	V12	2953	73 × 58.8	6 Weber	Marelli	Dunlop	4 disc	Ferrari 4 + rev.	aluminium	1000

The 1962 Le Mans 24 Hours.

1963

Race no.	Type	Engine position	No. of cyls & configur.	Capacity in cc	Bore & stroke/mm	Carburation	Ignition	Tyres	Brakes	Gearbox	Body material	Weight in kg
9	330 LM	front	V12	3967	77 × 71	6 Weber	Marelli	Dunlop	4 disc	Ferrari 4 + rev.	aluminium	
10	330 TR	front	V12	3967	77 × 71	6 Weber	Marelli	Dunlop	4 disc	Ferrari 4 + rev.	aluminium	
11	330 LM	front	V12	3967	77 × 71	6 Weber	Marelli	Dunlop	4 disc	Ferrari 4 + rev.	aluminium	
12	330 LM	front	V12	3967	77 × 71	6 Weber	Marelli	Dunlop	4 disc	Ferrari 4 + rev.	aluminium	1258
20	250 GTO	front	V12	2953	73 × 58.8	6 Weber	Marelli	Dunlop	4 disc	Ferrari 5 + rev.	aluminium	1074
21	250 P	rear	V12	2953	73 × 58.8	6 Weber	Marelli	Dunlop	4 disc	Ferrari 5 + rev.	aluminium	
22	250 P	rear	V12	2953	73 × 58.8	6 Weber	Marelli	Dunlop	4 disc	Ferrari 5 + rev.	aluminium	812
23	250 P	rear	V12	2953	73 × 58.8	6 Weber	Marelli	Dunlop	4 disc	Ferrari 5 + rev.	aluminium	812
24	250 GTO	front	V12	2953	73 × 58.8	6 Weber	Marelli	Dunlop	4 disc	Ferrari 5 + rev.	aluminium	
25	250 GTO	front	V12	2953	73 × 58.8	6 Weber	Marelli	Dunlop	4 disc	Ferrari 5 + rev.	aluminium	
26	250 GTO	front	V12	2953	73 × 58.8	6 Weber	Marelli	Goodyear	4 disc	Ferrari 5 + rev.	aluminium	1147

1964

Race no.	Type	Engine position	No. of cyls & configur.	Capacity in cc	Bore & stroke/mm	Carburation	Ignition	Tyres	Brakes	Gearbox	Body material	Weight in kg
14	330 P	rear	V12	3972	77 × 71	6 Weber	Marelli	Dunlop	4 disc	Ferrari 5 + rev.	aluminium	995
15	330 P	rear	V12	3972	77 × 71	6 Weber	Marelli	Dunlop	4 disc	Ferrari 5 + rev.	aluminium	963
19	330 P	rear	V12	3972	77 × 71	6 Weber	Marelli	Dunlop	4 disc	Ferrari 5 + rev.	aluminium	978
20	275 P	rear	V12	3299	77 × 58.8	6 Weber	Marelli	Dunlop	4 disc	Ferrari 5 + rev.	aluminium	945
21	275 P	rear	V12	3299	77 × 58.8	6 Weber	Marelli	Dunlop	4 disc	Ferrari 5 + rev.	aluminium	952
22	275 P	rear	V12	3299	77 × 58.8	6 Weber	Marelli	Dunlop	4 disc	Ferrari 5 + rev.	aluminium	940
23	250 LM	rear	V12	3286	77 × 58.8	6 Weber	Marelli	Dunlop	4 disc	Ferrari 5 + rev.	aluminium	955
24	250 GTO/64	front	V12	2953	73 × 58	6 Weber	Marelli	Dunlop	4 disc	Ferrari 5 + rev.	aluminium	1100
25	250 GTO/64	front	V12	2953	73 × 58	6 Weber	Marelli	Dunlop	4 disc	Ferrari 5 + rev.	aluminium	1083
26	250 GTO/64	front	V12	2953	73 × 58	6 Weber	Marelli	Goodyear	4 disc	Ferrari 5 + rev.	aluminium	1090
27	250 GTO/64	front	V12	2953	73 × 58	6 Weber	Marelli	Dunlop	4 disc	Ferrari 5 + rev.	aluminium	1077
28	250 LM	rear	V12	3286	77 × 58.8	6 Weber	Marelli	Dunlop	4 disc	Ferrari 5 + rev.	aluminium	949

1965

Race no.	Type	Engine position	No. of cyls & configur.	Capacity in cc	Bore & stroke/mm	Carburation	Ignition	Tyres	Brakes	Gearbox	Body material	Weight in kg
17	365 P2	rear	V12	4390	81 × 71	6 Weber	Marelli	Dunlop	4 disc	Ferrari 5 + rev.	aluminium	1003
18	365 P2	rear	V12	4390	81 × 71	6 Weber	Marelli	Dunlop	4 disc	Ferrari 5 + rev.	aluminium	996
19	330 P2	rear	V12	3977	77.1 × 71	6 Weber	Marelli	Dunlop	4 disc	Ferrari 5 + rev.	aluminium	1021
20	330 P2	rear	V12	3977	77.1 × 71	6 Weber	Marelli	Dunlop	4 disc	Ferrari 5 + rev.	aluminium	1013
21	250 LM	rear	V12	3285	77 × 58.8	6 Weber	Marelli	Dunlop	4 disc	Ferrari 5 + rev.	aluminium	951
22	275 P2	rear	V12	3285	77 × 58.8	6 Weber	Marelli	Dunlop	4 disc	Ferrari 5 + rev.	aluminium	
23	275 LM	rear	V12	3285	77 × 58.8	6 Weber	Marelli	Dunlop	4 disc	Ferrari 5 + rev.	aluminium	957
24	275 GTB	front	V12	3285	77 × 58.8	6 weber	Marelli	Dunlop	4 disc	Ferrari 5 + rev.	aluminium	1050
25	250 LM	front	V12	3285	77 × 58.8	6 Weber	Marelli	Dunlop	4 disc	Ferrari 5 + rev.	aluminium	963
26	250 LM	front	V12	3285	77 × 58.8	6 Weber	Marelli	Dunlop	4 disc	Ferrari 5 + rev.	aluminium	963
27	275 LM	front	V12	3292	71.1 × 58.8	6 Weber	Marelli	Goodyear	4 disc	Ferrari 5 + rev.	aluminium	966
40	Dino 166	front	V6	1592	77 × 58.8	6 Weber	Marelli	Dunlop	4 disc	Ferrari 5 + rev.	aluminium	600

1966

Race no.	Type	Engine position	No. of cyls & configur.	Capacity in cc	Bore & stroke/mm	Carburation	Ignition	Tyres	Brakes	Gearbox	Body material	Weight in kg
16	365 P2	rear	V12	4390	80 × 71	6 Weber	Marelli	Dunlop	4 disc	ZF 5 + rev.	aluminium	1029
17	365 P2	rear	V12	4390	80 × 71	6 Weber	Marelli	Dunlop	4 disc	ZF 5 + rev.	aluminium	1044
18	365 P2	rear	V12	4390	80 × 71	6 Weber	Marelli	Dunlop	4 disc	ZF 5 + rev.	aluminium	
19	365 P2	rear	V12	4390	80 × 71	6 Weber	Marelli	Dunlop	4 disc	ZF 5 + rev.	aluminium	1013
20	330 P3	rear	V12	3977	77.1 × 71	6 Weber	Marelli	Dunlop	4 disc	Ferrari 5 + rev.	aluminium	
21	330 P3	rear	V12	3977	77.1 × 71	6 Weber	Marelli	Dunlop	4 disc	Ferrari 5 + rev.	aluminium	981
25	Dino 206	rear	V6	1986	86 × 57	3 Weber	Marelli	Dunlop	4 disc	Ferrari 5 + rev.	aluminium	821
26	275 GTB	front	V12	3285	77 × 58.8	3 Weber	Marelli	Dunlop	4 disc	Ferrari 5 + rev.	aluminium	1183
27	330 P3	rear	V12	3977	77.1 × 77	6 Weber	Marelli	Dunlop	4 disc	Ferrari 5 + rev	aluminium	
28	275 LM	rear	V12	3285	77 × 58.8	6 Weber	Marelli	Dunlop	4 disc	Ferrari 5 + rev.	aluminium	980
29	275 GTB	front	V12	3285	77 × 58.8	3 Weber	Marelli	Dunlop	4 disc	Ferrari 5 + rev.	aluminium	1206
36	Dino 206	rear	V6	1986	86 × 57	3 Weber	Marelli	Dunlop	4 disc	Ferrari 5 + rev.	aluminium	
38	Dino 206	rear	V6	1986	86 × 57	3 Weber	Marelli	Dunlop	4 disc	Ferrari 5 + rev.	aluminium	722
57	275 GTB	front	V12	3285	77 × 58.8	3 Weber	Marelli	Dunlop	4 disc	Ferrari 5 + rev.	aluminium	1219

1967

Race no.	Type	Engine position	No. of cyls & configur.	Capacity in cc	Bore & stroke/mm	Carburation	Ignition	Tyres	Brakes	Gearbox	Body material	Weight in kg
19	P4	rear	V12	3982	77 × 71	Lucus fuel injection	Marelli	Firestone	4 disc	Ferrari 5 + rev.	aluminium	984
20	P4	rear	V12	3982	77 × 71	Lucas fuel injection	Marelli	Firestone	4 disc	Ferrari 5 + rev.	aluminium	972
21	P4	rear	V12	3982	77 × 71	Lucas fuel injection	Marelli	Firestone	4 disc	Ferrari 5 + rev.	aluminium	982
22	P3/4	rear	V12	3977	77.1 × 71	6 Weber	Marelli	Goodyear	4 disc	Ferrari 5 + rev.	aluminium	1001
23	P3/4	rear	V12	3982	77 × 71	6 Weber	Marelli		4 disc	Ferrari 5 + rev.	aluminium	1002
24	P4	rear	V12	3982	77 × 71	Lucas fuel injection	Marelli	Firestone	4 disc	Ferrari 5 + rev.	aluminium	976
25	P3/4	rear	V12	3982	77 × 71	6 Weber	Marelli		4 disc	Ferrari 5 + rev.	aluminium	997
26	365 P	rear	V12	4390	80 × 77	6 Weber	Marelli	Goodyear	4 disc	Ferrari 5 + rev.	aluminium	1027
28	275 GTB	front	V12	3286	77 × 58.8	3 Weber	Marelli		4 disc	Ferrari 5 + rev.	aluminium	1205

1968

Race no.	Type	Engine position	No. of cyls & configur.	Capacity in cc	Bore & stroke/mm	Carburation	Ignition	Tyres	Brakes	Gearbox	Body material	Weight in kg
14	250 LM	rear	V12	3286	77 × 58.8	6 Weber	Marelli	Goodyear	4 disc	Ferrari 5 + rev.	aluminium	
17	275 GTB	front	V12	3286	77 × 58.8	3 Weber	Marelli	Goodyear	4 disc	Ferrari 5 + rev.	aluminium + steel	965
19	275 LM	rear	V12	3286	77 × 58.8	6 Weber	Marelli	Goodyear	4 disc	Ferrari 5 + rev.	aluminium	934
20	275 LM	rear	V12	3286	77 × 58.8	6 Weber	Marelli	Goodyear	4 disc	Ferrari 5 + rev.	aluminium	984
21	275 LM	rear	V12	3286	77 × 58.8	6 Weber	Marelli	Goodyear	4 disc	Ferrari 5 + rev.	aluminium	956
36	Dino	rear	V6	1986	86 × 57	fuel injection	Marelli	Goodyear	4 disc	Ferrari 5 + rev.	aluminium	774

1969

Race no.	Type	Engine position	No. of cyls & configur.	Capacity in cc	Bore & stroke/mm	Carburation	Ignition	Tyres	Brakes	Gearbox	Body material	Weight in kg
17	250 LM	rear	V12	3285	77 × 58.8	6 Weber	Marelli	Goodyear	4 disc	Ferrari 5 + rev.	aluminium	970
18	312 P	rear	V12	2997	77 × 53.5	Lucas fuel injection	Marelli	Firestone	4 disc	Ferrari 5 + rev.	aluminium	878
19	312 P	rear	V12	2997	77 × 53.5	Lucas fuel injection	Marelli	Firestone	4 disc	Ferrari 5 + rev.	aluminium	859
59	275 GTB	front	V12	3285	77 × 58.8	3 Weber	Marelli	Goodyear	4 disc	Ferrari 5 + rev.	aluminium + steel	1220

The start of the 1969 Le Mans 24 Hours.

The 1970 Le Mans 24 Hours.

1970

Race no.	Type	Engine position	No. of cyls & configur.	Capacity in cc	Bore & stroke/mm	Carburation	Ignition	Tyres	Brakes	Gearbox	Body material	Weight in kg
5	512 S	rear	V12	4994	87 × 70	Lucas fuel injection	Marelli	Firestone	4 disc	Ferrari 5 + rev.	polyester	952
6	512 S	rear	V12	4994	87 × 70	Lucas fuel injection	Marelli	Firestone	4 disc	Ferrari 5 + rev.	polyester	936
7	512 S	rear	V12	4994	87 × 70	Lucas fuel injection	Marelli	Firestone	4 disc	Ferrari 5 + rev.	polyester	926
8	512 S	rear	V12	4994	87 × 70	Lucas fuel injection	Marelli	Firestone	4 disc	Ferrari 5 + rev.	polyester	924
9	512 S	rear	V12	4994	87 × 70	Lucas fuel injection	Marelli	Firestone	4 disc	Ferrari 5 + rev.	polyester	880
10	512 S	rear	V12	4994	87 × 70	Lucas fuel injection	Marelli	Goodyear	4 disc	Ferrari 5 + rev.	polyester	941
11	512 S	rear	V12	4994	87 × 70	Lucas fuel injection	Marelli	Goodyear	4 disc	Ferrari 5 + rev.	polyester	937
12	512 S	rear	V12	4994	87 × 70	Lucas fuel injection	Marelli	Firestone	4 disc	Ferrari 5 + rev.	polyester	916
14	512 S	rear	V12	4994	87 × 70	Lucas fuel injection	Marelli	Goodyear	4 disc	Ferrari 5 + rev.	polyester	942
15	512 S	rear	V12	4994	87 × 70	Lucas fuel injection	Marelli	Goodyear	4 disc	Ferrari 5 + rev.	polyester	926
16	512 S	rear	V12	4994	87 × 70	Lucas fuel injection	Marelli	Goodyear	4 disc	Ferrari 5 + rev.	polyester	915
57	312 P	rear	V12	2989	77 × 53.5	Lucas fuel injection	Marelli	Goodyear	4 disc	Ferrari 5 + rev.	polyester	812

1971

Race no.	Type	Engine position	No. of cyls & configur.	Capacity in cc	Bore & stroke/mm	Carburation	Ignition	Tyres	Brakes	Gearbox	Body material	Weight in kg
6	512 M	rear	V12	4993	87 × 70	Lucas fuel injection	Marelli	Goodyear	4 disc	Ferrari 5 + rev.	aluminium + polyester	950
7	512 M	rear	V12	4993	87 × 70	Lucas fuel injection	Marelli	Goodyear	4 disc	Ferrari 5 + rev.	aluminium + polyester	972
9	512 M	rear	V12	4993	87 × 70	Lucas fuel injection	Marelli	Firestone	4 disc	Ferrari 5 + rev.	aluminium + polyester	957
10	512 M	rear	V12	4993	87 × 70	Lucas fuel injection	Marelli	Firestone	4 disc	Ferrari 5 + rev.	aluminium + polyester	930
11	512 M	rear	V12	4993	87 × 70	Lucas fuel injection	Marelli	Goodyear	4 disc	Ferrari 5 + rev.	aluminium + polyester	957
12	512 M	rear	V12	4993	87 × 70	Lucas fuel injection	Marelli	Goodyear	4 disc	Ferrari 5 + rev.	aluminium + polyester	974
14	512 S	rear	V12	4993	87 × 70	Lucas fuel injection	Marelli	Goodyear	4 disc	Ferrari 5 + rev.	aluminium + polyester	986
15	512 M	rear	V12	4993	87 × 70	Lucas fuel injection	Marelli	Firestone	4 disc	Ferrari 5 + rev.	aluminium + polyester	953
16	512 M	rear	V12	4993	87 × 70	Lucas fuel injection	Marelli	Firestone	4 disc	Ferrari 5 + rev.	aluminium + polyester	945
58	365 GTB 4	front	V12	4390	81 × 71	6 Weber	Marelli	Goodyear	4 disc	Ferrari 5 + rev.	steel + aluminium	1514

1972

Race no.	Type	Engine position	No. of cyls & configur.	Capacity in cc	Bore & stroke/mm	Carburation	Ignition	Tyres	Brakes	Gearbox	Body material	Weight in kg
34	365 GTB 4	front	V12	4390	81 × 71	6 Weber	Marelli	Michelin	4 disc	Ferrari 5 + rev.	steel + aluminium	1365
35	365 GTB 4	front	V12	4390	81 × 71	6 Weber	Marelli	Michelin	4 disc	Ferrari 5 + rev.	steel + aluminium	1369
36	365 GTB 4	front	V12	4390	81 × 71	6 Weber	Marelli	Michelin	4 disc	Ferrari 5 + rev.	steel + aluminium	1402
37	365 GTB 4	front	V12	4390	81 × 71	6 Weber	Marelli	Michelin	4 disc	Ferrari 5 + rev.	steel + aluminium	1422
38	365 GTB 4	front	V12	4390	81 × 71	6 Weber	Marelli	Goodyear	4 disc	Ferrari 5 + rev.	steel + aluminium	1377
39	365 GTB 4	front	V12	4390	81 × 71	6 Weber	Marelli	Michelin	4 disc	Ferrari 5 + rev.	steel + aluminium	1445
46	Dino 246 GT	rear	V6	2418	92.5 × 60	3 Weber	Marelli	Michelin	4 disc	Ferrari 5 + rev.	steel + aluminium	1124
57	365 GTB 4	front	V12	4390	81 × 71	6 Weber	Marelli	Goodyear	4 disc	Ferrari 5 + rev.	steel + aluminium	1476
74	365 GTB 4	front	V12	4390	81 × 71	6 Weber	Marelli	Goodyear	4 disc	Ferrari 5 + rev.	steel + aluminium	1407
75	365 GTB 4	front	V12	4390	81 × 71	6 Weber	Marelli	Michelin	4 disc	Ferrari 5 + rev.	steel + aluminium	1385

Race no.	Type	Engine position	No. of cyls & configur.	Capacity in cc	Bore & stroke/mm	Carburation	Ignition	Tyres	Brakes	Gearbox	Body material	Weight in kg
6	365 GTB 4	front	V12	4390	81 × 71	6 Weber	Marelli	Goodyear	4 disc	Ferrari 5 + rev.	steel + aluminium	1350
15	312 P/B	rear	flat-12	2991	80 × 49.6	Lucas fuel injection	Marelli	Goodyear	4 disc	Ferrari 5 + rev.	polyester	692
16	312 P/B	rear	flat-12	2991	80 × 49.6	Lucas fuel injection	Marelli	Goodyear	4 disc	Ferrari 5 + rev.	polyester	692
17	312 P/B	rear	flat-12	2991	80 × 49.6	Lucas fuel injection	Marelli	Goodyear	4 disc	Ferrari 5 + rev.	polyester	690
33	365 GTB 4	front	V12	4390	81 × 71	6 Weber	Marelli	Michelin	4 disc	Ferrari 5 + rev.	steel + aluminium	1364
34	365 GTB 4	front	V12	4390	81 × 71	6 Weber	Marelli	Michelin	4 disc	Ferrari 5 + rev.	steel + aluminium	1451
36	365 GTB 4	front	V12	4390	81 × 71	6 Weber	Marelli	Goodyear	4 disc	Ferrari 5 + rev.	steel + aluminium	1353
37	365 GTB 4	front	V12	4390	81 × 71	6 Weber	Marelli	Goodyear	4 disc	Ferrari 5 + rev.	steel + aluminium	1354
38	365 GTB 4	front	V12	4390	81 × 71	6 Weber	Marelli	Goodyear	4 disc	Ferrari 5 + ev.	steel + aluminium	1370
39	365 GTB 4	front	V12	4390	81 × 71	6 Weber	Marelli	Michelin	4 disc	Ferrari 5 + rev.	steel + aluminium	1427
40	365 GTB 4	front	V12	4390	81 × 71	6 Weber	Marelli	Michelin	4 disc	Ferrari 5 + rev.	steel + aluminium	1412
56	365 GTB 4	front	V12	4390	81 × 71	6 Weber	Marelli	Dunlop	4 disc	Ferrari 5 + rev.	steel + aluminium	1342

The Dino in the 1974 Le Mans 24 Hours.

1974

Race no.	Type	Engine position	No. of cyls & configur.	Capacity in cc	Bore & stroke/mm	Carburation	Ignition	Tyres	Brakes	Gearbox	Body material	Weight in kg
1	312 P	rear	V12	2998		Lucas fuel injection	Marelli	Dunlop	4 disc	Ferrari 5 + rev.	polyester	782
18	Dino 308 GT	rear	V8	2926	81 × 71	4 Weber	Marelli	Goodyear	4 disc	Ferrari 5 + rev.	steel	1004
54	365 GTB 4	front	V12	4390	81 × 71	6 Weber	Marelli	Goodyear	4 disc	Ferrari 5 + rev.	steel + aluminium	1345
55	365 GTB 4	front	V12	4390	81 × 71	6 Weber	Marelli	Dunlop	4 disc	Ferrari 5 + rev.	steel + aluminium	1345
56	365 GTB 4	front	V12	4390	81 × 71	6 Weber	Marelli	Dunlop	4 disc	Ferrari 5 + rev.	steel + aluminium	1345
57	365 GTB 4	front	V12	4390	81 × 71	6 Weber	Marelli	Michelin	4 disc	Ferrari 5 + rev.	steel + aluminium	1378
71	365 GTB 4	front	V12	4390	81 × 71	6 Weber	Marelli	Michelin	4 disc	Ferrari 5 + rev.	steel + aluminium	

1975

Race no.	Type	Engine position	No. of cyls & configur.	Capacity in cc	Bore & stroke/mm	Carburation	Ignition	Tyres	Brakes	Gearbox	Body material	Weight in kg
47	365 GTB 4	front	V12	4390	81 × 71	6 Weber	Marelli	Michelin	4 disc	Ferrari 5 + rev.	steel + aluminium	1375
48	365 GTB 4	front	V12	4390	81 × 71	6 Weber	Marelli	Michelin	4 disc	Ferrari 5 + rev.	steel + aluminium	
17	308 GT 4	rear	V8	2926 2992	81 × 71	4 Weber	Marelli	Michelin	4 disc	Ferrari 5	steel	983
45	365 GTB 4	front	V12	4390	81 × 71	6 Weber	Marelli	Michelin	4 disc	Ferrari 5	steel + aluminium	1345
46	365 GTB 4	front	V12	4390	81 × 71	6 Weber	Marelli	Michelin	4 disc	Ferrari 5	steel + aluminium	1549
99	365 GT/4BB	rear	flat-12	4390	81 × 71	6 Weber	Marelli	Michelin	4 disc	Ferrari 5	steel	1351

1977

Race no.	Type	Engine position	No. of cyls & configur.	Capacity in cc	Bore & stroke/mm	Carburation	Ignition	Tyres	Brakes	Gearbox	Body material	Weight in kg
75	365 GT4BB	rear	flat-12	4390	81 × 71	Lucas fuel injection	Marelli	Goodyear	Lockheed disc	Ferrari 5 + rev.	steel	

1978

Race no.	Type	Engine position	No. of cyls & configur.	Capacity in cc	Bore & stroke/mm	Carburation	Ignition	Tyres	Brakes	Gearbox	Body material	Weight in kg
85	512 BB	rear	flat-12	4942	82 × 78	4 Weber	Marelli electronic	Michelin	4 disc	Ferrari 5	steel + polyester	1333
86	365 GT4 BB	rear	flat-12	4942	82 × 78	4 Weber	Marelli electronic	Goodyear	4 disc	Ferrari 5	steel + polyester	1166
87	512 BB	rear	flat-12	4942	82 × 78	4 Weber	Marelli electronic	Goodyear	4 disc	Ferrari 5	steel + polyester	1221
88	512 BB	rear	flat-12	4942	82 × 78	4 Weber	Marelli electronic	Michelin	4 disc	Ferrari 5	steel + polyester	1210
89	512 BB	rear	flat-12	4942	82 × 78	4 Weber	Marelli electronic	Michelin	4 disc	Ferrari 5	steel + polyester	1204

1979

Race no.	Type	Engine position	No. of cyls & configur.	Capacity in cc	Bore & stroke/mm	Carburation	Ignition	Tyres	Brakes	Gearbox	Body material	Weight in kg
61	512 BB	rear	flat-12	4942	82 × 78	Lucas fuel injection	Marelli electronic	Michelin	4 disc	Ferrari 5	steel + polyester	1198
62	512 BB	rear	flat-12	4942	82 × 78	Lucas fuel injection	Marelli electronic	Michelin	4 disc	Ferrari 5	steel + polyester	1258
63	512 BB	rear	flat-12	4942	82 × 78	Lucas fuel injection	Marelli electronic	Michelin	4 disc	Ferrari 5	steel + polyester	1227
64	512 BB	rear	flat-12	4942	82 × 78	Lucas fuel injection	Marelli electronic	Michelin	4 disc	Ferrari 5	steel + polyester	1187

1980

Race no.	Type	Engine position	No. of cyls & configur.	Capacity in cc	Bore & stroke/mm	Carburation	Ignition	Tyres	Brakes	Gearbox	Body material	Weight in kg
75	512 BB	rear	flat-12	4942	82 × 78	Lucas fuel injection	Marelli electronic	Michelin TRX	4 disc	Ferrari 5	pressed steel + polyester	1211
76	512 BB	rear	flat-12	4942	82 × 78	Lucas fuel injection	Marelli electronic	Michelin TRX	4 disc	Ferrari 5	pressed steel + polyester	1093
77	512 BB	rear	flat-12	4942	82 × 78	Lucas fuel injection	Marelli electronic	Michelin TRX	4 disc	Ferrari 5	pressed steel + polyester	1096
78	512 BB	rear	flat-12	4942	82 × 78	Lucas fuel injection	Marelli electronic	Dunlop	4 disc	Ferrari 5	pressed steel + polyester	1196
79	512 BB	rear	flat-12	4942	82 × 78	Lucas fuel injection	Marelli electronic	Michelin TRX	4 disc	Ferrari 5	pressed steel + polyester	1148

1981

Race no.	Type	Engine position	No. of cyls & configur.	Capacity in cc	Bore & stroke/mm	Carburation	Ignition	Tyres	Brakes	Gearbox	Body material	Weight in kg
45	512 BB	rear	flat-12	4942	82 × 78	Lucas fuel injection	Marelli electronic	Michelin TRX	4 disc	Ferrari 5 + rev.	steel + polyester	1102
46	512 BB	rear	flat-12	4942	82 × 78	Lucas fuel injection	Marelli electronic	Goodyear Eagle	4 disc	Ferrari 5 + rev.	steel + polyester	1130
47	512 BB	rear	flat-12	4942	82 × 78	Lucas fuel injection	Marelli electronic	Michelin TRX	4 disc	Ferrari 5 + rev.	steel + polyester	1102
48	512 BB	rear	flat-12	4942	82 × 78	Lucas fuel injection	Marelli electronic	Michelin TRX	4 disc	Ferrari 5 + rev.	steel + polyester	1107
49	512 BB	rear	flat-12	4942	82 × 78	Lucas fuel injection	Marelli electronic	Michelin TRX	4 disc	Ferrari 5 + rev.	steel + polyester	1078

1982

Race no.	Type	Engine position	No. of cyls & configur.	Capacity in cc	Bore & stroke/mm	Carburation	Ignition	Tyres	Brakes	Gearbox	Body material	Weight in kg
70	512 BB	rear	flat-12	4942	82 × 78	Lucas fuel injection	Marelli electronic	Michelin TRX	4 disc	Ferrari 5	steel + polyester	1115
71	512 BB	rear	flat-12	4942	82 × 78	Lucas fuel injection	Marelli electronic	Michelin TRX	4 disc	Ferrari 5	steel + polyester	1058
72	512 BB	rear	flat-12	4942	82 × 78	Lucas fuel injection	Marelli electronic	Michelin TRX	4 disc	Ferrari 5	steel + polyester	1084
73	512 BB	rear	flat-12	4942	82 × 78	Lucas fuel injection	Marelli electronic	Goodyear	4 disc	Ferrari 5	steel + polyester	1058

1984

Race no.	Type	Engine position	No. of cyls & configur.	Capacity in cc	Bore & stroke/mm	Carburation	Ignition	Tyres	Brakes	Gearbox	Body material	Weight in kg
27	512 BB	rear	flat-12	4990	83 × 78	Lucas fuel injection	Marelli electronic	Michelin	4 disc	Ferrari 5 + rev.	polyester	980

Photo Credits

AAT - Toscas : pages 133, 134, 135, 136, 137. — AFP : pages 8, 9, 16, 17. — Autef : pages 125, 126, 143, 144, 145, 149, 151, 152. — Autocar : page 13. — Autopresse / Archives Dominique Pascal : pages 7, 9, 10, 11, 13, 14, 16, 20, 21, 22, 24, 25, 26, 27, 28, 29, 30, 31, 32, 33, 34, 35, 36, 37, 38, 39, 40, 41, 42, 43, 44, 45, 46, 47, 48, 49, 50, 51, 52, 53, 54, 55, 57, 58, 59, 60, 61, 62, 63, 64, 65, 66, 67, 68, 69, 70, 71, 72, 73, 74, 76, 77, 78, 79, 80, 81, 82, 83, 84, 85, 86, 87, 88, 89, 90, 91, 92, 93, 94, 95, 96, 97, 98, 99, 100, 101, 102, 103, 104, 106, 107, 109, 110, 111, 113, 114, 116, 117, 118, 119, 120, 121, 122, 123, 124, 125, 126, 128, 129, 130, 133, 143, 146, 148, 149, 150, 155, 158, 159, 164. — Béroul : pages 12, 15, 17, 30. — DPPI : pages 90, 108, 109, 123. — Galeron : page 150. — L.A.T. : page 6. — Le Corre : pages 138, 139, 140, 141, 142, 143. — Ludwigsen : 13. — Morelli - Bertier : pages 112, 117, 121, 126, 144, 149, 166. — Photo Actualité : pages 112, 115. — Presse Sports : pages 24, 33, 34, 41, 56, 78, 101, 107, 123, 129, 130, 147. — copyright reserved: pages 9, 12, 15, 49, 55, 56, 70, 105, 113, 114, 147, 163.

Acknowledgments

The author wishes to thank all those who have helped in the preparation of this voluminous record; in particular Christian Moity, journalist with *Automobile Magazine* and historian of the Le Mans 24 Hours; also the press service of the ACO, in the persons of Monique Bouleux and Sylvie Chaudemanche.

• A big thank you, too, to the photographers who have captured on film those fleeting moments that after a few years take on the value of irreplaceable documents. Among them Maurice Louis Rosenthal, Philippe Dreux, Daniel Le Corre, Michel Morelli, Miltos Toscas, Michelle Bertier, Pierre Autef, Jean-François Galeron, Jean-Michel Dubois and Thierry Bovy, without whom this book would not have been possible.

• And, finally, my grateful thanks to my friends Serge Pozzoli, Peter Richley, Basil, Gilles and Louis for their friendly encouragement.

Achevé d'imprimer sur les Presses de Berger-Levrault à Nancy
en Janvier 1986
N° Imprimeur 778349-1-86
Dépôt légal Mars 1986
Imprimé en France